the
Entre
Spirit

the Entre Spirit

THE DNA OF SELF-STARTERS AND PEOPLE WHO GET THINGS DONE

BY MATT LAW

motus|press

Copyright © 2021 by Matt Law

Published in Orange City, Florida, by MotusPress.

All rights reserved. No part of this book may be reproduced in any form or by any electronic or mechanical means including information storage and retrieval systems, without permission in writing from the author and publisher. The only exception is by a reviewer, who may quote short excerpts in a review.

For more information about the author, please visit *EntreSpirit.com*.

Special discounts are available on quantity purchases by corporations, associations, and others. For details, contact the author by visiting the website listed above.

First Printing: 2021 MotusPress
First Edition

ISBN 978-0-9992176-2-7

Printed in the United States of America

9 8 7 6 5 4 3 2 1

For Sarah, my best friend, partner, and wife. Thank you for joining me on the many crazy adventures our lives have brought us. Your kindness, love, and faith in me have made me the man I am today.

This is a work of fiction. The characters represented in these pages do not reflect the actions or personalities of real people. Similar namings of companies, characters, situations, or events are purely coincidental and do not reflect reality. Though we have faced similar adversities, our experiences and how we came up with this fable are explained in the Afterword.

1 THE ACCIDENT

Wham! Luke's head smashed against the overhead bunk as he woke up in a tizzy. The unwelcome banging on the door coming from the top deck had startled him. Trying to make sense of it all, he rubbed his temples as his eyes opened, and the room came into a blurry view. Why was he sleeping in the crew cabin? More importantly, who was on his boat so early in the morning—and how did they get down here? Though awake for only a few seconds, he could feel his anger welling up inside. With his head throbbing and eyes watering, a second, even louder notice was given, followed by the chime of the doorbell. Gathering himself and aiming for the stairs, his one objective was to stop the awful racket. Standing up so quickly made the tiny cabin spin and reminded him that he had way too much to drink. Knocking over a bottle of Jack Daniels and a half-eaten bag of potato chips didn't help. His rage exploded as he reached the port side stairs, pointing to mid-deck. By the time Luke arrived at the sliding glass door of the luxurious sailboat, he realized he was only wearing his black and white checkerboard boxers, but he decided not to care.

"Who is it? And please stop knocking!" Luke yelled in a demanding voice as he yanked the curtains back, expecting a cleaning lady—arriving way too early.

"Officer Ramos—Miami Dade Sheriff's Office. I apologize for the early morning notice, sir. Your wife told me I could deliver the papers down here."

Outside stood a petite brunette woman with a baseball cap, blue jeans, and a floral-patterned blouse. Her strong and confident tone demanded respect, though her stature was no more than five foot two. With the permission of Luke's wife, she had made it through his home, past the dock, and onto the 78-foot catamaran to which he had escaped for the last three nights. The silver badge hanging around her neck and the .40 caliber pistol she sported on her right side made Luke quickly apologize for his appearance. His awkwardness continued as he clumsily attempted to cover himself with the translucent curtain and signed his name to receive the envelope.

Though he'd been expecting the visit, it didn't make it any easier. He thought about his company and his business partner every day, but whenever the sheriff's office showed up, he knew the pain would be that much worse. While they were always courteous, it embarrassed Luke to have gun-wielding policemen at his home. Closing the sliding glass door, he now caught a glimpse of his reflection. His forehead glowed a bright Rudolph red—a reminder of the dangers of sleeping on the bottom bunk. Luckily, he connected with the board straight-on and hoped there wouldn't be a bruise.

Continuing to the galley and hovering over the coffee pot as if to speed it up, Luke's shoulders slumped as his mind drifted back. It had been eighteen months since the tragic accident that changed everything. In an instant, his best friend and partner, Dellin Betanchio, was dead, and his beloved company lay in ruin. As the CEO and co-founder of CataSail Yachts Incorporated, Luke had built the catamaran manufacturer into a thriving $400-million enterprise. The envy of its rivals, CataSail dominated the world of luxury catamarans and was expanding just as things took a turn for the worse. When news of the accident made national headlines, neighbors, friends, and most customers were quick to blame him for the epic disaster. The press called for Luke to resign.

Investors called for him to man up. Regardless of who said what, he couldn't save the company, and he now carried this heavy burden.

Luke sighed as he focused his attention down at the lifeless manila envelope, still sealed shut on the counter. Though he already knew what was inside, he stood motionless, contemplating when he would open it. Then, to prepare himself, he sucked in a deep breath, almost like a child before diving to the bottom of a swimming pool. Tearing off the top and flipping to page two, he silently began to read—*JROB Holdings, LLC versus Luke D. Voightmann*. Luke released the trapped air as he continued scanning the document. His investors were finally going after him for a grand total of $79 million. The absurdity of the amount made him roll his eyes as he thought about the men he once called friends.

Judge, Romine, Ottavino, and Bird were the four private equity partners from lower Manhattan who formed JROB Holdings. The new LLC swooped in on CataSail's Series B financing, buying out the other investors and becoming the company's third-largest shareholder behind Luke and Dellin. Over the years, these men had dined with Luke, sat on the company's board, and profited greatly from CataSail's success. However, after the accident, relationships began to sour. A request for an increase in the company's line of credit was met with strong opposition. JROB Holdings wanted to stop the expansion efforts in light of the accident. Luke refused, stating that any delay in construction would cost CataSail several million dollars in interest and penalties. With both sides firmly entrenched, the holding company finally agreed to increase the credit line but required Luke's personal guarantee. After six weeks of searching for alternative financing without success, Luke reluctantly signed for the debt in hopes things would turn around. Unfortunately, the media embellished the accident with all sorts of rumors which further devastated the company.

Slamming the lawsuit on the counter, Luke shook his head in disbelief. It no longer mattered how much money JROB Holdings wanted—or for that matter, what anyone wanted. CataSail was finished.

Knowing his investors would be coming after him, Luke had already liquidated almost everything he owned. Piece by piece, his kingdom of power and glory vanished before his eyes. As each asset sold, a piece of Luke went with it. The first memento to go was the three-bedroom waterfront condo on Miami Beach. The impeccable unit was wiped clean, listed, and under contract in just five days, causing him to regret selling it so cheaply. Next to go was his beloved mountain getaway, a thirty-acre North Georgia estate that served as the family's winter lodge. Within three weeks, two more treasured vacation spots were either sold or under contract. Three single-family rental homes and a duplex were also listed and disposed of. Luke cashed in the little he had left in his investment accounts and sold his 911 Turbo S convertible—a painful day indeed for any Porsche enthusiast. All that remained was his house and the money from selling everything he owned. Sixteen million dollars might sound like a lot of money, but that, along with his waterfront home, would also be gone once JROB Holdings was finished with him.

More than just his possessions, the aftermath impacted every crevasse of Luke's life. His proud title of Chief Executive Officer had been stripped away. He was no longer a young hip boss, a smart businessman, or for that matter, anyone important. He was plain old Luke D. Voightmann, just another failed entrepreneur riddled with insecurity. Neglecting his health and turning to alcohol, Luke isolated himself from the outside world. He stopped answering his phone and deleted his social media accounts. The truth is, Luke didn't want to be encouraged by well-meaning friends, and he certainly didn't want to talk about CataSail or Dellin. Instead, he buried his pain deep inside, trying to block out everything that reminded him of his previous way of life. To escape his troubles, Luke spent most afternoons on his CataSail yacht docked outside. Though it was a bitter reminder of his past, it provided him a place of solitude—at least until the sheriff's office took that too.

A distant chime from Luke's cell phone somewhere on the deck below brought his attention back to the present. Realizing his coffee was ready, he poured a cup and focused on his pounding head. Unsure if it was a hangover or his collision with the top bunk, popping four ibuprofens in his mouth and washing them down with a sip of coffee was his first attempt to be pain-free. What happened last night? After his last drink, everything was a bit fuzzy. Where were his clothes and why was he sleeping in the crew cabin? Luke decided it didn't really matter and headed down the starboard stairs to the master suite.

Within a few minutes, he was dressed in a pair of blue surfer shorts, a white T-shirt, and a pair of black flip-flops. He continued getting ready by combing down his thick, wavy hair and shaping his flowing beard. The six-foot, thirty-seven-year-old was now but a shadow of the handsome man he used to be. No longer interested in eating healthy or going to the gym, he quickly packed on fifty pounds of delivery pizza and Chinese. His skin color even seemed to change. The countless afternoons spent sulking in the sun darkened it, causing Luke to look like a Spanish-speaking native of Miami. Without anywhere to go each day, Luke lost all motivation to maintain his appearance. He neglected his barber, and for that matter, all essential grooming. The former clean-cut and fit CEO had somehow transformed. Almost like an intentional disguise, his tan skin, added weight, long hair, and beard now made him unrecognizable to most.

After a quick inspection in the mirror, Luke opened the drawer of his nightstand, grabbed a small prescription bottle, and shoved it into his right front pocket. He then unplugged his phone and headed for the stairs. Reaching the top, he briefly paused to contemplate where he might pass the time. Outside of the large picture windows, the cloud-filled sky offered morning shade, and he thought about sitting outdoors. Convinced the covering might keep the South Florida heat at bay, he opened the glass door and headed upward—coffee cup in hand to fight off his hangover. Reaching the top deck, he sat down at the helm to take in the views of his beloved home on Palm Island.

Of all of his possessions, Luke loved his home the most. Its modern design and bright white paint made it unique among the island's Mediterranean theme. While not the biggest house in the neighborhood, the modern architectural appeal made up for what it lacked in size. With floor-to-ceiling windows and sweeping views of the port, it had a way of mesmerizing everyone who entered. Situated opposite of the cruise terminals on Biscayne Bay, one was almost guaranteed to see a passenger-loaded ship float by on any given day. The outdoor spaces and infinity pool completed the home and made it an ideal, year-round playground for a rich, young Miami businessman. It was good for business too. With a large dock and its proximity to the shipyard, it was the perfect spot for entertaining clients receiving delivery of their new yachts. For years, CataSail celebrated these momentous occasions by throwing extravagant christening parties and inviting the "who's who" of Miami. These events were famous on the island, carrying on through the house, the pool deck, and onto the new yachts. Though Luke's wife didn't particularly enjoy the high-profile living, she liked that her husband's commute was just six miles away.

Feeling slightly more alert, Luke unlocked his phone and started compulsively deleting the many voicemails he had received since yesterday afternoon. He didn't need to listen to the sixteen new messages—he knew they were all from corporate collection companies. At first, Luke tried to be civil and politely explain to the callers that the company had folded. They didn't care though and persisted in badgering him day in and day out. He stopped taking their calls when he realized he couldn't reason with these people. He even considered changing his number but opted to keep it so friends could stay in touch. *Where are all my friends now?* he thought as he finished deleting the voicemails and moved on to his text messages.

The first text was an automated shipping confirmation—probably something Meredith had ordered. The second text came from Luke's attorney, Doc Ahmad, stating that he'd be calling a little later to discuss the lawsuit. Finishing up, Luke placed his phone next to him on the soft captain's chair. With his hand still resting on the back of it, another text arrived. The message was from Luke's wife that simply read:

Hey! I'm guessing you got the package. I'm so sorry! I know this might be a hard day for you, but I'm here if you need me. Maybe we could talk about everything tonight?

Luke exhaled a deep breath as he thought of Meredith and their argument from a few nights ago. By the time the fight was over, he was headed for the boat docked outside, his bags packed in a fiery fit of rage. For the first time in their marriage, the couple didn't sleep together in the same bed. Nor did he tuck his young kids in. Instead, Luke sat in a drunken stupor for nearly seventy-two hours, putting a further strain on his marriage. Now, his sober mind rehashed the words Meredith had spoken that set him off. From what he could remember, she suggested giving up the house because her parents were willing to let them stay at their condo until they got back on their feet. If that wasn't enough, she even mentioned putting the kids in public school and going back to work.

Her attempt to help her husband was taken as an insult, and Luke—already half-lit from a few beers—responded by hurling his own hurtful advice. "Are you serious, Meredith? What are you telling them? If I can build a $400-million company, I think I can figure this out! If you want to help, just give me some time to think and get off my back, would ya?" Now seeing things in a slightly different light, he felt bad for his terrible behavior.

Luke took another sip of coffee and exhaled a deep breath as if letting out a giant puff of cigarette smoke. Thankfully, the ibuprofen was kicking in and starting to alleviate his headache. Slowly slouching down and propping his legs up against the control center, his stomach now protruded and created the perfect platform for his coffee cup. Before he could fully relax, the sound of a tour boat in the distance caught his attention. Though still some twenty yards away, he could hear the tour guide mention his starkly unique home on the loudspeaker. It was the same speech on every tour.

As the boat drifted from sight, Luke let out a big yawn and closed his eyes. Before he could nod off, a seemingly enormous drop of water found its way down from the bottom side of the roof and managed to land directly inside his left ear. "Oh, come on!" he said with a startle as if the water droplet could hear him. Shaking his head to remove the water was a terrible idea. Still recovering from last night's binge and his top bunk collision, his headache returned with a vengeance, throbbing pain in rhythm with his pulse. Adding to the insult, a large fresh spot of black coffee now decorated his white shirt. "Give me a freaking break!" he mumbled as he tried to wipe the coffee off of his stained shirt. Remembering the anxiety meds in his pocket, he opened the pill bottle, popped in two pills, and washed them down with all that remained of his coffee.

Within a few minutes, the meds were helping Luke relax. Staring off at the terminal, the sounds of diesel engines, backup beeps, and foremen shouting instructions in Spanish played in unison as four-passenger cruise ships were made ready for departure. Seeing the boats caused Luke's mind to travel back in time again. This time, he thought of the Saturday afternoon barbecue that took place a week before the accident. Dellin and his family had come over to celebrate the launch of the R48—CataSail's newest high-tech catamaran. Leaving their wives to watch the kids by the pool, the two men escaped to the quiet top deck of the sailboat to celebrate over bottles of beer. As they spoke quietly, a highly intoxicated tourist in the distance was set on getting their attention. Yelling and swinging his shirt over his head didn't exactly show his purpose, but no doubt the man was having a good time and excited about his upcoming cruise and balcony cabin.

"Imposter!" Dellin jabbed with a slight Spanish accent that came out when he was passionate or had a buzz. "He wouldn't know luxury cruising if it hit him between the eyes." For six minutes, Dellin continued to rant about how CataSail's luxury was far superior to any cruise ship experience. "These imposter tourists and all the new mega cruise ships are ruining our industry. Flank steaks and domestic wine wrapped up with piss-poor service, and they're celebrating like they're having the time of their lives. They are imposters, not tourists! Mix them together and you get impurists," Dellin said. He had created a new word, and it stuck in Luke's mind like a pickaxe. It would be their last conversation.

The following week, Dellin and a staff member sailed the new yacht to Baltimore's Inner Harbor, where he was to deliver it to Senator Urshela and his family. Normally, one of the staff captains would have taken the delivery, but Dellin insisted on doing it himself because of the important buyer and wanting to see how the new boat handled on the Atlantic. The plan was to arrive on Friday and spend Saturday showing the yacht while in port. For whatever reason, CataSail's crew and Senator Urshela's family sailed out of the harbor and onto the Chesapeake early Saturday morning. As they reached the middle of the bay, the unthinkable happened.

The fire and the explosion that followed claimed everyone's life, with the exception of the senator's eleven-year-old grandson, who happened to be sitting on the trampoline netting at the bow of the vessel. Thankfully, he was wearing a life vest when the blast knocked him unconscious, threw him overboard, and saved his life. Within minutes, nearby boaters pulled the boy from the chilly November waters. As he regained consciousness, the boaters realized who he was and that Senator Urshela had been onboard the engulfed boat. Within minutes, helicopter media crews hovered over the smoking wreckage, capturing the final images of the Coast Guard searching for bodies as the boat went under.

The media coverage and investigation that followed brought Cata-Sail to its knees, blacklisting the brand from all potential yacht buyers. Reporters, cameramen, and photographers swarmed in, literally camping outside of Luke's home and business. Within a month, legal fees mounted, and fifty-five percent of existing orders were canceled. Without Dellin managing operations, the company went into a tailspin as continual meetings with lawyers filled Luke's calendar. Threats of class-action lawsuits and countless calls from customers demanding refunds plummeted the company's morale. Within sixty days, all existing orders were

2 ROOTS
HOW IT ALL STARTED

The sound of two women speaking nearby awoke Luke from his dreamland. Swiveling around in his chair, he spotted Friday's cleaning crew wiping the glass that surrounded the pool deck of his home. A glance at the control center clock told him the morning had reached 10:18. With nothing but time to spare, his mind traveled back again to his best friend and partner. Out of everything he'd lost, losing Dellin impacted him the most.

The two young men met during their freshman year at MIT. Luke spotted Dellin's Florida Marlins hat across the dining hall, which sparked their first conversation. Within minutes, they concluded they'd grown up just an hour apart and were both obsessed with Miami's professional baseball team. An instant friendship was formed, and by the start of their sophomore year, the two became nearly inseparable. Dellin, a computer science major, was at times extremely introverted. On the other hand, Luke studied business and could often be loud and outgoing. Despite their different personalities and majors, the two seemed to blend together, allowing them to hang out for hours without getting on each other's nerves. Soon, they were closer than brothers—rooming and studying together and experiencing MIT's unique parties. When summertime came around, they hung out at each other's homes. Luke even joined Dellin's family on a two-week vacation across Europe.

With such a close friendship, it was only natural that they would talk about business from time to time. The problem was that neither one had a good idea. That is, until the day they returned to Boston Harbor after a long day of sailing. The trip that was supposed to be an epic experience on a new catamaran ended up being unremarkable for the two technology nuts. It started as just a seed, but by the time they were done talking that night, CataSail was a full-blown idea. The pull for Luke and Dellin, two college seniors with entrepreneurial dreams, couldn't be contained. Skipping out on parties and extracurricular activities, they eliminated everything they could, allowing them to meet and talk about CataSail.

While excited about the idea, they knew their families might not be happy with their decision to start a business. This realization became crystal clear when Luke's girlfriend dumped him a week after he shared his plans. Dellin also took a gamble and shared CataSail with his older brother. After being shot down harshly, his brother reminded him of the cost to attend MIT and their parents' expectations. The idea of creating a sailboat company and all that entrepreneurship entailed was mystifying for so many. It meant they'd be skipping grad school and leaving MIT without the expected—and almost guaranteed—high-paying jobs. Though both were unsure of the future, they were determined to at least give it a shot. They celebrated completing the business plan and vowed to keep CataSail a secret until they could explain it the right way. The night before graduation would be a perfect time to break the news, as both families would be in town to celebrate.

As the big announcement approached, the young men masterfully planned the event, leaving no room for their parents to veto the idea. A venue was chosen overlooking the harbor. From the nautical-themed meeting room to the carefully selected seafood menu, the young men calculated every detail. The invite cards for the dinner were sent to their siblings, parents, and grandparents. Most understood it would be a typical graduation dinner for the two friends celebrating a milestone together.

By six o'clock, all twenty-three family members had arrived and were seated at two rectangular tables. A beautiful sunset toasted the guests, who were already a little happy from the abundance of wine.

As they finished eating and the waiter took orders for coffee and dessert, Luke and Dellin quietly excused themselves. Returning with a projector, retractable screen, and a sealed cardboard box caused a buzz of excitement to come over everyone. No one had expected a speech, let alone a presentation from the two graduates. Not by coincidence, they began by sharing a picture slideshow, set to their parents' favorite music, which included happy memories from everyone in the room. They then humbly thanked their parents and grandparents for the many sacrifices made in life that now allowed them to graduate from college. With the entire audience now endeared to the charming young men, they were ready to share their big idea.

For the next twelve minutes, Luke and Dellin eloquently and passionately communicated their first catamaran design, just as they had rehearsed it a half dozen times before. Assisted by digital sketches and video animations, the presentation was flawless in every way. It mesmerized the now more serious audience—who also seemed slightly confused with what was happening. Bouncing back and forth with each slide transition, they poured out the statistics, details, and why the world needed a new sailboat company. Their enthusiasm even caught the imagination of a busboy passing by.

As they neared the end of the presentation, Luke loaded the final slide, revealing the CataSail logo. Dellin popped the lid off a cardboard box and began removing the spiral-bound business plans. On cue, one of the servers carted in a miniature model of the new CataSail 1000. Luke then said the words that would change these two friends' destinies forever. "I hope you are all as excited as we are about the possibilities of entrepreneurship. Dellin and I are pleased to present our new company and future—CataSail Yachts Incorporated!"

The awkward silence seemed to last an eternity as the vulnerable men awaited the verdict. Instant panic, along with a whirlwind of malicious thoughts, attacked both of them as they started breaking down the equipment—a clear signal they were finished. *Maybe we shouldn't have surprised them with this. Do they even like the idea? Was the big ending a little too much? Does Mom truly grasp I'm not going to grad school? Does Dad realize I won't be getting a job? Worse yet, does anyone realize that starting next Monday, we don't have a place to live?* It was a huge gamble to hide their plans and wait for graduation, knowing it could have easily backfired.

Whether the family understood the ramifications or not, it no longer mattered. Standing up together and fervidly applauding, they'd given the boys the endorsement they desperately wanted. Proud tears filled the eyes of the women, and firm handshakes abounded with the men. The celebration continued as Uncle Domingo, the entrepreneur of Dellin's family, kissed and hugged Dellin for nearly ten seconds. The rest of the family followed. Like a receiving line for a bride and groom, each member came forward to bless the young duo and inspect the sailboat model. To top this happy occasion off, the young men found out that CataSail would have a hundred grand to get started, a generous graduation gift from the boys' parents.

The first decision for CataSail was to figure out where they'd locate the business. Though Boston had technology and shipbuilders, what the boys needed was a place to live and work for free. It didn't take long for both of them to conclude that Dellin's family home in Coral Gables would be the perfect spot, if they could get his parent's approval. Located right on the water, the sprawling mansion offered a 3,900-square-foot detached guest suite, complete with a private entrance, game room, and a two-car garage. If the boys really needed to impress a client, the main house could also be used for meetings, as Dellin's parents were often traveling and seldom there. Thankfully, the empty nesters were more than happy to offer the space to the boys.

Two days after graduation, Luke and Dellin were packed and headed south on I-95. They planned to spend a week at the Voightmann's home in West Palm, discussing business with Luke's father, before continuing to Dellin's place. As a child, Luke never really understood what an investment banker was or how his dad could do this sort of thing from home. As fate would have it, Dave Voightmann was well connected and agreed to help them raise money for CataSail. After finely tuning their business plan and setting clear objectives, they headed south to Coral Gables, ready for action.

Though Luke and Dellin had an ideal situation for starting the business, they didn't take it for granted. Working morning, noon, and night, they planned out every detail of the company. Within four months of setting up camp at Dellin's house, they had three purchase contracts for the CataSail 1000. Thanks to the internet and their ability to communicate their ideas, the combined total sales would reach $4 million—that is, if CataSail could deliver the boats. With the help of Luke's father, the young men began pitching angel investors, hoping to get enough capital to push their plan. Their relentless confidence, the new boat sales, and MIT degrees helped them close on an equity infusion to the tune of $20 million—$5 million more than they needed. As the money flowed in, Luke and Dellin went to work securing a lease, hiring staff, and connecting with suppliers. Two more boat orders came in from investors who were excited about the company's future.

CataSail's initial success wasn't due to their clever brand but the harmonious relationship between the two young men—Dellin building the boats and Luke building the company. As CEO from day one, Luke brought marketing and creativity to the table. His intuition and drive allowed him to sniff out opportunities and capitalize on them before others. Though Luke loved the sun and sailing, he knew next to nothing about building boats when they started. It was the company's COO, Dellin Betanchio, who was the true shipbuilding expert. Dellin had been sailing Florida's waters since his seventh birthday when his father purchased a new, eighty-two-foot yacht. To Dellin's delight, the boat manufacturer's CEO was a close friend of the family and allowed him to hang out in the shipyard from time to time. By age fourteen, Dellin worked weekends, prepping the boats for delivery and installing final touches. At fifteen, he was helping nearly twenty hours a week, doing small mechanical work and wiring electronics.

As everyone hoped, CataSail's launch and new boats were a huge success. Driven by innovation, they were one of the firsts to build "smart yachts"—a big deal back then. Their proprietary system allowed the boat's owner to manage the entire ship from a small touchscreen tablet. The lighting, temperature, and even the ship's autopilot system could be monitored and controlled through this new technology. With an average length of over sixty feet, CataSail's catamarans also packed a tremendous amount of living space inside their two lower compartments. Most models could easily sleep eight with additional quarters for the crew. Spacious ensuite bathrooms and far-reaching picture windows trademarked the below-deck cabins. Ample storage, solar-powered deep freezers, and freshwater makers made the boats ideal for long-distance cruising.

At last, Luke and Dellin's hard work was paying off, allowing them to reach the Inc. 5000 list at breakneck speed. More attention followed when they were named the fastest-growing, privately-held yacht company in America. By their third year in business, an eighteen-month waiting list ensured success, and the company doubled its expansion efforts, allowing them to build ships even faster. Due to increasing demand, CataSail raised their prices and started requiring full payment upfront, giving them more cash for expansion and allowing them to pay dividends. As they entered year four, a group of investors known as JROB Holdings approached Luke, asking him to create a second round of funding for CataSail. They practically threw money at the company, buying out the other investors and making Dellin and Luke multi-millionaires. CataSail had mastered the art of building luxurious, high-tech sailboats, but not every critic praised their success or labeled them as purebred entrepreneurs. Hanging over their head was their families' wealth, Luke's investment banking father, and their shiny MIT degrees. All of these were clear factors in the company's success, but few realized how fervently the two young men had worked to bring life to their vision.

Coming in with the money and fame was a herd of desperate women looking to land a rich young husband. Thankfully, long hours at the shop kept the men away from the gold diggers at Miami's club scene. However, the disadvantage of being so busy was that Luke and Dellin remained single longer than most bachelors their age. Though they both had relationships from time to time, they never seemed to last long once their girlfriends realized the men's true affection was CataSail. Both sets of parents applied pressure, hounding Luke and Dellin to settle down, work a little less, and get married. The men often joked that the only thing their parents really wanted from them was grandchildren.

This supersonic pace came to a screeching halt two days before Dellin's twenty-sixth birthday, when his father suddenly dropped dead from a heart attack. It shocked everyone, as Dellin's father had just turned seventy-two, was in decent health, and still performed cosmetic surgery a few days per week. The death hit everyone at CataSail hard and taught Dellin and Luke how fragile life could be. Both men vowed to start working less and enjoy life more. True to their words, they brought on additional staff, including several new foremen, managers, admins, and a bright young chief marketing officer. Dellin hired an experienced operations manager who had been building boats for twenty years. Luke dumped all the marketing onto the new CMO and delegated most of his research and planning to a new executive assistant. The new hires pulled their weight, and within six months, both men's schedules could easily sustain a forty-hour workweek.

Dellin, deeply grieving the death of his father, began searching for contentment outside of CataSail. After studying for six months to get his pilot's license, he purchased a Cessna 400 and started taking weekend trips across the Caribbean. When his mother mentioned selling the family home in Coral Gables, he immediately offered to buy it. Though the home made his commute twenty minutes longer, the waterfront property allowed a seaplane to reach the Caribbean even faster. Dellin also started boxing again, one of his father's passions and something he hadn't done since high school. Most importantly, he started seeing his future wife,

Adriana Morales, a long-time friend of the family. The two reconnected at the memorial service for Dellin's father. Six months into their relationship, he proposed on a beach in Cozumel, and the two were quickly wed in a small private ceremony. Deeply committed to keeping a limited work schedule, Dellin took at least eight weeks of vacation every year. When the company's growth demanded more from him, he simply hired more staff.

On the other hand, Luke's drive and competitive spirit wouldn't let him rest. Everywhere he looked, there was an opportunity for the company to improve, and he quickly found other ways to stay busy. Within six months of bringing on the new support staff, he was back to working long hours, immersed in the next big thing. He couldn't help but live and breathe CataSail. To him, it was his rite of passage as a start-up CEO. He carried the burden for the company, his employees, and investors on his shoulders. Like a machine, Luke pushed the business forward. When it stumbled, he picked it up, threw it on his back, and kept moving.

Triple-digit growth and accolades fueled his fire. Featured articles published in industry magazines about CataSail's remarkable growth made the hard work worth it. Winning Miami's Entrepreneur of the Year Award further sealed Luke's relentless addiction to achievement. CataSail's staff honored their CEO's efforts by throwing him a huge birthday party, celebrating Luke's day and CataSail reaching $100 million in annual sales. JROB Holdings praised the CEO's efforts with each dividend check they received. Even outside investors wanted in, often approaching CataSail with inquiries about investing. In his glory, Luke happily dismissed them as too late in the game. CataSail didn't need their money and was already on its way to becoming something great.

The sound of police sirens coming from the MacArthur Causeway captured Luke's attention. Sitting up slightly, he spotted the flashing blue lights of an unmarked car and SUV headed towards beachside. As the vehicles traveled out of sight, he slouched back down, concluding there wasn't anything worth watching. The sun now scorched the roof of the catamaran, making him sweat profusely. Starting to get thirsty, he remembered the mini-fridge located a few steps away. *Was there a bottle of water in there?* Celebrating his score by flipping off the lid, he took a swig and plopped back onto the captain's chair. As he wiped the dripping sweat from his chin, he thought of his wife and how she hated his beard. For the last couple of months, Meredith had begged him to shave it off, telling him he looked like Tom Hanks from the film *Cast Away.*

Luke sighed as his mind traveled backward again. This time, he pictured his wife and the day they first met. His younger sister, Catherine Chelsey, or known by her family as CC, had invited him to join her and a group of friends kayaking during spring break. Though living just ten miles from Luke and attending the University of Miami, CC barely saw her brother due to his busy schedule. Of course, Luke didn't really want to take a day off to go kayaking with a bunch of strangers, but he decided to come as a peace offering for being a lousy big brother. Pulling up to the outfitter, he immediately noticed Meredith—an attractive brunette standing around five foot seven. She was talking to CC as they waited for the rest of the group to arrive. Fortunately for Luke, the others who were supposed to come kayaking didn't show up that day, allowing some room for him to get to know Meredith better.

As Luke approached the ticket counter, he knew he wanted to ask her out and planned his strategy. He'd set up his sister and get her to ask about CataSail. He'd respond with a few outrageous numbers and nonchalantly mention his new Aston Martin convertible. If Meredith didn't know anything about cars, he'd go on a rant about how hard it was to get insurance for such a fast vehicle. He'd then invite his sister over for dinner next week to see his new oceanfront condo. If there were still no bites, he'd ask CC if she had any suggestions for vacations and that he was considering Paris or Rome. With a mental checklist ready, he moved in.

Unfortunately, Luke's plan didn't quite work out as expected. As they launched their kayaks, he got a good look at Meredith's face when he nearly capsized. Splashing and flailing to recover, he soaked everyone around, including Meredith and his sister. Thankfully, Meredith laughed it off, thinking his dramatic scene was simply a joke. Seeing her smile,

Luke froze with an awkward and longing stare. CC noticed it right away and later told him he looked like a desperate little boy wanting a puppy. For the next three hours, Luke tried his best to start a conversation with Meredith as they paddled along. To his dismay, she seemed uninterested in talking about his business. More so, she maneuvered her kayak to the other side of CC and focused the conversation back on the plethora of fish. Luke would probably have given up, but as he studied her more closely, he couldn't help but be intrigued by her self-assuredness. Meredith's blue eyes, spunky curly hair, and bold confidence seemed so different from the girls he'd met before.

As they returned to the outfitter's dock, panic struck the now more insecure CEO, who realized he knew next to nothing about this mysterious girl. From bits and pieces of their dialogue, he gathered she was also raised in West Palm Beach, twenty-one years old, and about to graduate. As Meredith turned in her lifejacket and headed for the bathroom, Luke grabbed his sister's arm, keeping her from following her friend. He had but a few seconds to get the information he desperately needed.

"Don't leave me hanging, sis! What's the story with your friend Meredith? She's pretty cute!" he said, his grin giving away how interested he was.

"Ha ha! I knew you liked her! No offense, bro, but I think she's outta your league," CC responded, shaking his hand off of her elbow. "She's too good for you anyway. She's not a party girl and doesn't date around. She goes home on the weekends, attends church, and studies all the time. Unless you're going to become an altar boy or something, I don't think you've got a chance."

Ignoring CC's response, Luke continued looking for an angle. "Does she know anything about me? I mean, have you told her about me before? Does she think I'm cute? Come on, sis, help me out here!"

"You're so pathetic, dude. You got a thousand girls after you. Why do you want to date my friends? I don't know if she's interested in you. She's never asked me about you, so I doubt it. She knows you own a boat company, but that's it, I guess—" CC cut her response short as Meredith rounded the corner.

Now within earshot, CC continued with a laugh. "Hey, bro, here's your chance. Why don't you ask her yourself, Rico Suave?"

"Ask me what?" Meredith asked naively as CC passed by with a smile and headed to the bathroom.

Luke, extremely embarrassed by CC's comments, tried to cover up the awkward moment and said, "Oh, she's just a little crazy. It's not her fault though—our parents dropped her a lot when she was little."

Thankfully, Meredith thought Luke's comment humorous, giving him the courage to continue. Regardless of the outcome, it was now or never. "Seriously though, she's always trying to set me up with people. Anyway, she thought you and I might go well together. So, I was wondering if you're free next Friday or Saturday night. I'd love to take you out to dinner or something, maybe lunch, or coffee, or maybe a movie. You know, just to get to know you a little better." The words left Luke's mouth in such an awkward way, almost as if it was his first time asking a girl out, but he didn't know if he'd get another chance.

Meredith smiled calmly, not seeming particularly excited about the invitation. Scratching her head, she said, "Hmmm. Let me think about that. Next weekend? Let's see…I'll be home for my brother's birthday party and spending time with my family. Let me talk to them and figure out my schedule. Maybe I can get back to you through your sister, if that's okay?"

"Sure…no problem!" Luke said as his face turned red out of embarrassment, feeling like he'd just been shot down. She didn't want his number and she didn't give Luke her number. It was the old, "I'll get back to you through your sister" routine. Indeed, Meredith's confidence was unlike anything he'd seen in a woman before. She wasn't throwing herself at him. She didn't seem to care about his money or title. If she did, she sure didn't let Luke know. She was a mystery, and whatever she had, Luke wanted it. Fortunately for Luke, she did think he was cute. And after talking to CC to learn more about his character, she finally agreed to let him have her phone number, but only after making him wait two grueling weeks.

Luke soon realized that Meredith was truly a family girl, spending almost every weekend at home. Brought up by conservative parents, the only thing that seemed to matter to her was her family and faith. It was intimidating for Luke, but he realized if he wanted to see Meredith, it meant being with her family as well. Over the next two months, Luke spent his Saturdays driving to West Palm to see Meredith and getting to know her family. For the ten months they dated, he picked her up at four and dropped her off by midnight—no exceptions. Then he made the trek back to Miami. By seven o'clock the next morning, he was on the road again, this time, driving to meet Meredith at church. Though his friends teased him about his girlfriend's strict parents, Luke didn't care. For the first time in his life, he was starting to work less, and he was falling head over heels in love. By his twenty-seventh birthday, the two were married. Three years later came David, their oldest son. Two years after that, little Pauly was born.

For the better part of ten years, life went pretty well for the Voightmanns, and many thought Luke to be an ideal husband. Unlike some of his peers and college classmates who were promiscuous, Luke remained faithful to his wife and considered himself a happily married man. Each night, the couple had the same routine. After tucking their kids into bed, they retreated to the pool deck, talking for hours over a glass of wine. Being a father also seemed to come naturally to Luke, who, by his own admission, could get a bit out of hand when he was with his sons. Wherever his family went, they seemed to always be giggling, wrestling, and knocking things over, causing Meredith to joke about needing a babysitter for her husband. Though his schedule was often unpredictable, Luke did his best to be home every night. If he had to work late and missed dinner, he made up for it at bedtime, tickling his kids until they nearly peed their pants.

Luke exhaled another deep breath as he shook his head in regret. It wasn't intentional, but somehow, his effort to save the company had made him a stranger in his own home. Granted, nobody sets out to ruin their marriage or neglect their kids, but after the accident, he simply didn't know what else to do. Day after day, he woke up before the sun came up and kept working until midnight. Then he'd come home, kiss his sleeping children and wife, and do it all over again. He gave everything he had in one last-ditch effort to save CataSail. When he couldn't, he exhaustedly fell into despair. Like a dark shadow, the heaviness of his failures followed him everywhere he went. His only remedy for the pain was sitting alone on his sailboat each afternoon, drinking beer, and wallowing in his misery. Though physically present most nights, he was emotionally absent, subconsciously pushing his family and everyone else far away.

Meredith had carried on, managing their home and family. Of course, she was mourning Dellin and CataSail too, but that's not what grieved her the most. What broke her heart was her husband's self-destructive behavior. Luke knew something had to change. He also knew he didn't deserve his wife's affection, and if she wanted to, she easily could leave him. His actions since the accident certainly deserved it. On top of that, they were losing everything, and if she stayed, it certainly wasn't for the money. Despite Luke's best effort to self-sabotage, Meredith had remained steadfast. She was grounded and balanced—so warm and kind. She was so good, and he was—well, none of those things, at least not anymore.

📍 3 THE DARKEST OF DAYS

A few minutes after eleven, Luke's phone rang. Lifting the device, he could now see the caller ID, which read, Arturo Ahmad—corporate attorney. Arturo, also known as Doc by his friends, had handled CataSail's legal affairs for more than a decade. Doc's expertise made him an invaluable asset to Luke and his team. Not only did he manage the company's investor relations, but he was also a trusted advisor. No matter the issue, Doc seemed to always know what to do and how to fix any problem. More than just a professional, he was also a dear friend to both Luke and Dellin—even attending both of their weddings. He had been through thick and thin with Luke, helping him fight the politically driven lawsuits and standing next to him the day Dellin was buried. Doc was the type of guy who was always there. Though he was a straight shooter, he had a way of delivering the most terrible news with warmth and even the slightest bit of optimism.

Clearing his throat, Luke professionally greeted his caller as if to show he had no idea who was calling. "Hello. Luke Voightmann speaking."

"Luke, It's Doc Ahmad. You got a minute to chat?"

"For you? Sure, I do. How are you, man?" Luke opened the dialogue, sounding far more positive than his situation allowed.

"I'm good, Luke. Listen, I know we've got a meeting coming on Monday, but I'd like to talk to you before you get here. JROB Holdings forwarded me a copy of the lawsuit, but I also got a call from their attorney. Can we talk about this right now?" Though Doc called Luke often, today, his tone seemed a bit more serious.

Without hesitation, Luke said, "You sound stressed, Doc. Come on, man! It can't be that bad! We knew the lawsuit was coming. What's changed since last week?"

Doc continued, "Well, you're not going to like it, but it's getting pretty nasty. They know you're sitting on your cash and are ready to fight. They also know that we can tie them up for years, and there are some ways you can shelter your assets. Obviously, they don't want that. By chance, have you spoken to any of them?"

"Anyone at JROB Holdings? No way! We had a conference call that went south right before we closed, but you already know about that. That's when it all hit the fan. They wanted payment on the line, and I told them I had to make payroll instead. We closed a month later. There have been a few emails, but nothing over the last few months. Nothing from their attorneys except the letters. Why are you asking, Doc? What's changed?" Luke nervously responded as he waited for Doc to share the news.

This time, Doc didn't hold back. "They want an uncontested judgment. No fighting or defense case. More than anything, they want you to hand over all your cash, including the deed to your home, within fifteen days, or they're planning to bring a criminal lawsuit against you. I asked them for what, and they said for fraud and embezzlement. I know—"

"Fraud and embezzlement? Are you kidding me?" Luke exploded as he stood up and began pacing back and forth across the deck, his anger now boiling against the investors he once called friends. "That's total bullshit, man, and you know it! Of all the idiotic things I've heard in my life."

"I know. I know it is," Doc said, trying to ease his client's concerns. "From what I've seen, your books are squeaky clean. I don't think they have a case, but today's call made me a little concerned for you. Their attorney mentioned your sailboat. He was pretty convinced that you could be charged for stealing it from the company. It's a bully move and borderline blackmail, but they're trying every stop to get your assets."

"What a load of crap! In all the years of working with these guys, never did I think it would come to this. They've sat and had dinner on this boat with me. They know good and well it belongs to the company! I've had it with this garbage. Who's to say I can't sue them for trying to blackmail me?" Luke's outrage spilled over as he contemplated declaring war on JROB Holdings.

Well aware of Luke's rage, Doc slowed the pace and softened his tone. "Listen, I'm sorry, and I get why you're upset. I really do—especially after all you've gone through. Let me share with you a few things, and then you can think about it over the weekend, maybe talk to Meredith, and we'll figure it out from there. For starters, let me clarify what they want. The paperwork you received today is for a creditor's lawsuit. That's a simple way for them to get their money. If we don't fight it, it will only take them a couple of months to get the final judgment and seize your assets. Again, that's if we don't fight them. However, if we do fight the lawsuit, well, the truth is, it will take much, much longer. It could be years and years before they get their hands on anything. There's also a chance they could lose and end up with nothing."

"So, what's changed then? The last time we spoke, you told me the lawsuit was coming, but we could fight, stall, and appeal them to death. You said there were lots of options. I don't get it, Doc." Entering CEO mode now, Luke turned the confrontation to the lawyer, applying the same pressure he would a staff member who didn't deliver on their word.

"That's why they're threatening criminal charges. They want to bully you, Luke. They want you to stop fighting and give up. JROB Holdings is a different type of animal. They've hired some serious brass and are going for blood. They want your cash, your house, and everything you've got left—right now. No contest. No appeals. No fighting. Nothing but your unconditional surrender. The other lawsuits you have are small potatoes compared to this one. Those are just credit card companies. They play by a different set of rules. We can delay those all day long. They're so small that you could even pay them all off and still be set for life, but this is different. I want to be sure you understand the magnitude of what JROB Holdings is suggesting."

Doc paused and took a sip of something, giving Luke a chance to respond.

"I can't believe I'm even having this conversation," Luke said passionately. "The boat belongs to the company—not me! They know that! They also know that even if I sold it for $20 million, the company would have still folded. It's probably worth $7 million max, and that's if I found a buyer in the first place. Do they want the boat? They can have it! My ass is sitting on it right now! They can take it away and try to sell it themselves."

"That's the thing, Luke. You closed the company, all while keeping it docked at your home. Now you've got a $7-million catamaran that could have been sold with the proceeds going into the company. It could at least pay some of your creditors. I know that even if you found a buyer for the boat, the company would have still closed, but they'll use the fact you didn't try to sell it against you. They'll say you tried to steal it and keep it for personal use. Those guys are smart, and they'll twist the story. All I can say is that they seem to think they've got enough to convict you. The call was nasty today, and I think you and Meredith need to at least talk about it."

Luke sat back down at the helm—exasperated by the conversation and now at a loss for words. The shock of the moment was reminiscent of the day he learned Dellin had passed.

Hearing Luke's heavy breathing, Doc continued in a calm tone. "I'm sorry, Luke. I know this isn't good news, but let me explain how this might go. If they try a criminal lawsuit, their legal team will dig up all the dirt they can find on you. They'll build a case for the state of Florida by talking to past employees, customers, and anyone who has anything bad to say about you. They'll package it up nice and pretty and hand everything to the state's attorney on a silver platter. They'll likely leak partial truths and bald-faced lies to the press, which could gain attention and cause the state to investigate. If the state feels pressure from public opinion or finds fault in your actions, they could bring criminal charges against you. It could be an ugly mess and that's why I had to call you today."

Luke finally understood the magnitude of the conversation. Now, in the most sarcastic tone, he confirmed his options. "So, let me try to understand this. I either lay down and die, letting the vultures take everything I have left, leaving me homeless, or I go to jail for nothing? That's just great! Half the world still thinks we killed Senator Urshela anyway—of course they're going to want my head on a platter."

"Honestly, I don't think they want to bring criminal charges," Doc said softly, trying to reassure his client. "If they wanted you locked up in the Florida State Prison, why would they call me today? So I could warn you? I don't think so. Clearly, they're after your assets. You personally guaranteed their note, so I believe they're just hoping you'll surrender everything without a fight. Please don't stress it. At least not yet. All I'm saying is it's just something you need to be aware of. I'm going to call a few friends who specialize in criminal defense and get their take. I'll have more information by our meeting on Monday. Make sense?"

"Luke? You there? Hello—Luke, you still with me?"

After a few seconds, Luke finally responded—his mind adrift in the confusion. "Yes, sorry, Doc. I'm here. Just trying to understand everything. I'll think about this more and talk to Meredith. I appreciate you calling me and letting me know. Is there anything else?"

"Nothing else that really matters, my friend. Hang in there. We'll get this figured out. This is nothing for the good doctor. Are you doing all right besides all of this? How are Meredith and those boys? I bet they're getting huge!" Knowing the burden that Luke carried, Doc couldn't help but worry about his friend.

Luke's response was void of emotion. He simply didn't want to talk anymore. "They're good. Getting bigger all the time. Listen, I've gotta run. I'll see you on Monday. Thanks."

The conversation was over, and Luke was left with nothing but his imagination to run wild. Slowly lowering himself onto the deck, Luke laid down face first. The lawsuit, Doc's call, and his trip through his past were more than he could bear. With arms wrapped around his head and his lips touching the boards, Luke wept bitterly as the slow-motion picture played of him being hauled away in handcuffs. Would he be brave for his onlooking family or cry like a baby? Like a lost little boy in a busy shopping mall, Luke felt utter hopelessness. It was entrepreneurship that brought him here, a crazy roller coaster ride that turned into a living hell filled with demonic creatures and horrific nightmares. Why hadn't he seen its dangers? Understandably, Luke wished he'd never gotten on the ride in the first place. Feeling no longer valuable to the world, he was content to die—waiting for creditors, the police, or the morgue to take his body away. Not even his happy pills could stop him from the depression and ugly thoughts that surrounded him.

Had things continued like this for much longer, Luke probably wouldn't have made it. He might have died from alcohol poisoning, suicide, or simply a broken heart. However, sometimes there's a turning point in life—a moment in time where one can pinpoint exactly where they were when things began to shift. Luke's moment to remember was him lying down, face first, bawling like a baby on the top deck of a catamaran. He was thirty-seven years old, $79 million in debt, and unemployed. His friend was dead, his company destroyed, his marriage strained, and if that wasn't enough, he could be tried for embezzlement. There, lying down in the Florida heat, drenched in his tears, alone with his thoughts at precisely 11:33 on a Friday morning, momentum started to shift. The moment was so quiet and unobtrusive that he wouldn't recognize it for at least a week. Nonetheless, the life-changing moment started when his phone chimed the "choo-choo" sound—a special tone reserved only for text messages from his wife.

Worried that Meredith might have seen him from the pool deck—or worse yet, heard his wailing—he quieted his tears and reached for his phone. Slowly crawling back into his chair, he was relieved to see that she wasn't sitting outside, and his meltdown had remained confidential.

Meredith: *Hey. There's some guy here in a black SUV asking for you. He says he has an important invitation. I asked him to leave it, but he said he has to personally hand-deliver it to you. I told him I'd check with you.*

Luke: *You've got to stop answering the door! I have no idea who it is. It could be anyone. Private eye? Attorney? Press? Don't let him in!*

Meredith: *Don't worry, babe! I didn't. The chain is still locked on the door. I'm good! I thought it was my package. Sorry! Give me a minute, and I'll try to figure out what this is about. I didn't know if you were expecting him.*

Luke: *No. I don't know who it is.*

Meredith: *Okay, so he says you've been invited by a Mr. Stanton. He has a big golden envelope in his hand and says he must hand-deliver it to you...not your wife. He said he can come back later today if that is easier for you.*

Luke: *Strange. Stanton, huh? You sure he has the right house?*

Meredith: *He said Luke Voightmann and he mentioned CataSail.*

Luke: *What does he look like? It's probably some scam or something.*

Meredith: *IDK. Tall. Black. Spanish accent. Nice suit. I don't know, what do you want me to do? HE IS WAITING...HELP!*

Luke: *Please stop answering the door! You're killing me! I am not even fully dressed yet. I can't see him like this. Can you ask him to come back this afternoon? Maybe around four, and I'll come up there to meet him? I don't want him down here.*

Meredith: *Okay, 2 secs.*

Meredith: *Okay. He said he'll be back between 4 and 4:30 and left his card. He asked if you could call him if you weren't going to be here. I'll send you a pic of his card in a second. Please don't be mad at me. I thought it was a delivery. I kept the chain on, at least. That's progress, right?*

Luke: *Okay. I will come up a little later. BTW, I feel bad about what I said the other night, and I wanted to say I'm sorry for being a jerk yet again. I had a pretty heavy call with Doc today, and we need to talk about it. Please tell the boys I miss them and will see them soon.*

Meredith: *Okay. I'm headed to lunch with CC before I go to the school. I'll be back around 2:30ish. I'm sorry too. I know a lot is going on with the lawsuit, but we'll figure it out.*

Luke's phone chimed one more time when Meredith sent the picture of the visitor's business card. It was plain white and void of a logo, website, or any of the details a business card would usually have. Luke read it out loud as he Googled the card's owner. "Miguel Chapman. Personal Assistant. Stanton Enterprises." *Hmmm...let's see what Google says about you, Miguel.* The search results came up empty, and without a company website or email address on the card, Luke wasn't sure of the legitimacy of his guest. The Stanton name did seem familiar, but he couldn't quite pinpoint it. The lack of information about the situation began to annoy Luke, and without further thought, he began to dial the number on the card, hoping for clarity.

The call rang once and then went straight to voicemail. Luke almost hung up when he heard a man speaking Spanish on the other end but decided to listen a little longer. Thankfully, the voice also provided an English translation of the message.

"You've reached the voicemail of Miguel Chapman. Please note, I handle only the personal affairs for Mr. Stanton and his family. For calls relating to any of our companies, including Stanton Yachts, Stanton Apparel, or Stanton Fishing, please hang up and dial the company directly. If you're returning a call, please leave a message at the tone—beep."

Luke hung up the phone, now realizing that today's visitor was somehow connected to his past. Stanton Yachts was the company that purchased a couple of CataSail's designs and patents a few days before they closed. He'd never met the people over there though because his assistant had negotiated the terms of the transaction. But what did they want from Luke? Though Meredith said it was some sort of invitation, Luke wondered if the visit was related to their deal. Maybe they had some questions for him. Or maybe they wanted him to make some changes to the boat designs. Though Luke had no intention of accepting any invitation or helping the company, he was thankful the man had come. It offered him an excuse to be in his home. Despite his new burden, he longed to see his sons and to be close to his wife again.

"Excuse me, Mr. Voightmann! Could we clean the boat now, sir?" a female voice rang out from below. Two housekeepers with carts in tow stood at the end of the dock. After finishing the main house, they were ready to tackle the boat. Waving for them to approach, Luke assumed Meredith was probably gone and he could enter the main house. As he stood up and stretched over the railing, he addressed the approaching women.

"Is my wife gone?" he asked, hoping for the green light to enter.

"Yes, sir. She left a couple of minutes ago," one of the maids answered.

Luke nodded and quickly retreated from the top deck, passing the ladies as they entered the boat. By one o'clock, Luke showered and was dressed in khaki pants and a plaid dress shirt. Confident that people living in Florida should wear flip-flops, he slipped his feet back into his favorite pair as he headed for the kitchen. After a few minutes of searching, a tall ham sandwich, a bag of Doritos, and a glass of iced tea accompanied him as he sat down in front of his computer. Though seldom used, Luke's second-story office was his favorite room in the house. The natural light of the afternoon sun poured into the room's floor-to-ceiling windows, making it warm and cheerful. Now freshly cleaned, the polished desk and fingerprint-free glass reminded him of how much he loved his home.

With at least an hour and a half before his family returned, he decided to go through a stack of mail that had accumulated over the last few days. One by one, each letter was discarded until he came to the fourth letter in the stack. Inside, a small handwritten notecard read:

Dear Luke,

Today, I was going through some old pictures, and I found this one. I know how special this day was for both of you. I wanted you to have it as I know it will bless you. We are doing well. Of course, we miss our Dellin, but Adriana and the kids are going to be fine.

We think about you often. I hope you can bring your family to see us soon. Maybe you could plan a trip this summer when they are out of school. I hope to hear from you soon.

Love Always,
Mama Betanchio

Slowly flipping over the included old photo revealed a memory that was forever tattooed into Luke's mind. Standing tall and proud are two young men with huge grins on their faces. Between them, they proudly display the CataSail 1000. They're shaking hands and holding the old CataSail business plan. It was the night before graduation, and the two naive entrepreneurs were ready to tackle the world.

Luke sat back in his chair as he smiled at the picture. Lifting his feet onto the desk, he thought back to that momentous night. Standing there were two dumb but happy kids. They didn't know what they were doing, but they were thrilled to be on the adventure. Looking at their skinny faces and remembering their immaturity made Luke smile. Despite his terrible day or his seemingly impossible situation, the picture and note warmed his heart. Maybe it was the bright cheery room that changed his disposition, or perhaps it was the time spent waiting for his family to arrive home. Maybe it was the assurance that some people still loved him, or the relief one feels after bawling their eyes out. Though he didn't really know why, he was feeling a little better.

4 A MILLION-DOLLAR OPPORTUNITY

"Daaaaddy? You home?" the five-year-old yelled out loud as he flung open the front door. "Are you in here, Daddy?"

"I'm up here, Pauly, but only if you can find me. This time, I'm hiding really good!" Luke replied as he stood up to hide, acknowledging the game of hide-and-seek was on.

Pauly hunted for his father with his little footsteps echoing up the concrete stairs. The boy's counting commenced in the form of a song, indicating that his dad better hide, or else. "1...2...I'm gonna find you, 3...4...behind the door, 5...6...no more tricks, 7...8...gonna set you straight, 9...10...let's do it again!" The little rhyme was Pauly's favorite song, and finding his dad was one of his favorite adventures. Now reaching the top of the stairs, he finished his counting and began tiptoeing towards Luke's office—a common hiding space in times past.

"I'm gonna find you, Daddy. Then you in biiiig twouble. You didn't tuck me in last night," the boy continued as he peeked into the office. Carefully inspecting the space, he looked under the desk and behind the door as he continued the verbal discipline of his father. "I'm gonna find you, Daddy. I know you're in here." On to the ensuite bathroom, the boy marched but came up empty. Next, he checked the attached closet, another common hideout. Luke wasn't there either. This would now be an epic hunt for the child, whose confidence continued to grow as he taunted his father out loud. "You aren't in here, Daddy, but I'm gonna find you."

Though outwardly the boy mirrored his mother, inwardly, his spirit was kindred to Luke's, and he seemed to always prefer his father. His curly brown hair and bright blue eyes made him more handsome than most children his age, but what attracted people to little Pauly was his passionate personality. When happy, the little performer sang, bounced, and jumped everywhere he went, infecting those around him with laughter. On the other hand, when he didn't get his way, red hot rage, spit, and tears erupted in an instant, causing his parents to secretly nickname him their demon child.

Luke hid quietly in the hall closet opposite his office as he heard Pauly's little feet pass by again. Now growing a little tired of the game, the boy asked for his dad's help. "Daddy? Where are you? I can't find you! Gimme a hint!"

Eager to assist and get out of the closet, Luke clumsily banged the door, giving away his location. When the door sprung open, Luke knelt on one knee as Pauly jumped into his arms for a big hug. Tickling, followed by laughter, made the boy instantly forget not being tucked in as he shouted, "I found him, Mommy. I win again!"

Carrying the hyper boy on his shoulder and tickling him on request, Luke headed downstairs to his wife. Still in mom-mode, Meredith ignored him as she put away her keys and unpacked the boy's Spiderman lunchbox. After finishing the job at hand, she finally turned to acknowledge her husband, giving him the smallest of smiles. Luke continued to tickle little Pauly. It wasn't much, but it was the smallest sign that said he wanted to be a better father and husband.

"Where's David?" Luke asked softly.

"Did you forget? He's camping with the Cub Scouts at Baggs Cape this weekend. I dropped him off after school. I told you—"

"Oh man, I totally forgot that was today!" Luke interrupted as he lowered the giggling child to the floor. Kneeling beside his son, he put his hands on the boy's shoulders and said, "Could you do me a huge favor, Pauly? I need you to watch Spiderman for me, buddy, and tonight, you can tell me all about it when I tuck you into bed. I need to talk to Mommy for a few minutes."

Though not wanting to leave his father, the pull to watch Spiderman was too great for his young mind, and the boy quickly vanished. Meredith shouted after him, "No soda, little man! No soda!" referring to the refrigerator stocked with beverages in the media room.

Now alone in the kitchen, Luke leaned over the large granite island that separated the couple. Inspecting each other in silence, they waited a moment to ensure the child was gone. Luke slowly stretched his hand across the counter. After taking a deep breath, he looked up at his wife and said, "I'm sorry, babe. I know I screwed up again. Can you ever forgive me?"

Though most knew Meredith as a tender, soft-spoken mother who preferred a quiet life, Luke knew another side of his wife. When pushed to her limit or taken advantage of, a fiery side could come out, and Luke learned a long time ago that his CEO title didn't mean anything at home. As a mother, she demanded respect and obedience from her children. When she had to raise her voice, which wasn't very often, the kids knew she meant business, and even Luke could become a little scared of her. But this time, Luke hadn't just crossed the line—he obliterated it. Hidden in a drunken stupor for the last three nights, he completely ignored his wife and kids. And if there was ever a time he deserved his wife's wrath, it was today.

Meredith stood silently, looking down at the countertop. After exhaling, she quietly whispered, "Something's got to give, honey. We have to figure it out because I just don't know what else to do. I feel like I'm losing you and I hate it. I miss you. The boys miss you. You're just not yourself, and I'm worried about you—sitting around on that boat all day with nothing to do. This isn't the Luke Voightmann I married."

"I know, and I'm so sorry. I've been such a mess lately. I don't know what's wrong with me and why I can't get over all of this. I feel like I have a good day, and then, out of nowhere, something comes up, and I get stuck in a rut. I'm going to do a better job, but I need to know we're okay."

Meredith nodded, slowly extending her hand to Luke's, saying, "We're okay. But, you better figure something out, Luke Voightmann! I mean it! We have to make some changes." Then, without cracking a smile, she changed her voice to mimic little Pauly's words, and said, "Or else you'll be in biiiig twouble, Daddy! Biiiig twouble."

Taking her hand, Luke laughed as he pulled his wife around the island. As he embraced her, he said, "I know, I know. I have issues. Everyone knows that. Seriously, I'm so sorry for what I said the other night. I know you're worried. I am too." Luke's willingness to be vulnerable was just what Meredith needed.

Deeply missing her husband, she pulled back slightly to look him in the eyes and said, "I'm sorry too. I shouldn't have said so much the other night either, and you're right—I do need to get off your back."

"No! I'm the one who was wrong," Luke interrupted as he pulled his wife close again. "I just need to calm down."

Pulling away slightly, she again looked him in the eyes and said, "Well, I've been thinking a lot about it today. This season has been hard on us—and especially you. We've lost the company, and then we had to sell everything! And then there's Dellin—" When Meredith spoke Dellin's name, her bottled up tears poured out.

Seeing his wife's sorrow cut Luke's heart, and his eyes also began to soften with tears. He held her close until he could compose himself to continue. "We all miss him! I don't know why it has been so hard for us, but I'm sick of all this, and I'm ready for a new season. Maybe you're right, and moving into your parents' condo would be good for us. I don't know."

"Are you kidding me, Luke Voightmann—we are NOT moving! You love this house and we're staying here until they kick us out!" Meredith said passionately as she wiped the tears from her face.

With their oldest son away for the night and little Pauly consumed by a movie, the couple continued the conversation outside, sitting in their favorite two loungers on the shady pool deck. When Luke shared about JROB Holdings' plan to incriminate him, Meredith became unglued. Siding with her husband, her fire returned as she considered the sinister move by the investment group. Luke was a lot of things in life, but a thief wasn't one of them. The mere mention of Luke stealing the boat after how hard he had worked infuriated Meredith. Luke calmly tried to set his wife's mind at ease, explaining their options and encouraging her that Doc was working on it. Feeling affirmed by his wife's support, Luke opened up further about his struggles, speaking sorrowfully about how much he missed his family, his friend, and CataSail. Meredith couldn't hold back her tears. For the first time in eighteen months, it was as if she'd unlocked her husband's broken heart. They continued talking until there were no more words to say, quietly holding hands, sipping iced coffee, and watching the afternoon waterway.

At precisely 4:07, the doorbell rang. Not wanting the moment to end, Luke let out a small grumble as he remembered the visitor from earlier in the day. "Let it go, honey! Let's ignore him and maybe he'll go away. I'm not going to wherever he's inviting me anyway. I just came up here to be with you. Besides, this is your fault. If you hadn't answered the door in the first place, I wouldn't have to talk to this guy," Luke said jokingly as he reached for his wife's elbow.

Meredith, already standing, wasn't about to be influenced by her now more jovial husband. She quickly jabbed back in a sarcastic tone that only she could use with him. "Ha! You're so rude, Luke Voightmann. You know I thought it was my package. And you're not my boss. Move your butt! He's here. You're here. And you're talking to him."

Reluctantly, Luke stood up and the couple headed through the living room and kitchen until they came to the foyer. As Meredith reached for the door to greet the visitor, Luke poked her in her side. Making a face and pointing to the peephole, he was intent on training his wife on the proper and safe way to answer the door. A quick look revealed the same visitor from earlier in the day. Meredith rolled her eyes at her husband, affirming she understood his instructions and that everything was safe. She continued to torment him by ever so slowly removing the chain and carefully opening the door as if he had taught her to do the impossible.

Outside stood Meredith's previous visitor, a handsome, tall black man, which the couple assumed to be in his late forties. He wore a tailored black suit with a solid white shirt visible beneath his jacket. Though the man lacked a tie, his appearance was nonetheless impeccable. His finely pressed shirt and polished black shoes mixed with an air of self-confidence demanded respect.

"Hello again!" Meredith greeted the visitor.

"Hello, ma'am," said the man in a smooth Spanish accent. Now smiling, his white teeth contrasted his dark black skin, making him even more handsome.

"I'm Miguel Chapman of Stanton Enterprises. Are you Mr. Luke Voightmann?"

"I am," Luke responded—unsure of what to make of the formal introduction. "How can I help you?"

"I am here to present you with this," answered Miguel as he handed Luke the golden envelope. "We invite you to join us in a very special contest of entrepreneurs, Mr. Luke. Please read everything, sir."

Unsure of what to say, Luke opened the envelope and scanned the contents. Before he could finish reading it, Miguel said, "If you'd like, take a little time and discuss everything with your wife. I can wait outside for you. Just come back when you have a decision for me."

Whatever was in the envelope became very interesting to Luke. He didn't look up or acknowledge the visitor's words as he continued reading everything again. Pausing briefly, he opened a folded piece of paper which caused his eyes to light up. He then said softly, "This says I have to give you a decision by six o'clock tonight. Is that right?"

"I'm sorry for the late notice, sir. Our team came by last week and no one was home. We also call you, but no one pick up. I am sorry, Mr. Luke, but we are at the last moment to join as contest starts on Monday. Maybe you talk with your wife and let me know?"

"Talk about what? What's starting on Monday?" Meredith said, not yet privy to the contents of the envelope.

"Yes, a few minutes to talk in private would be good," Luke said as he closed the invitation and handed it to his wife. "Could you give us fifteen minutes to discuss everything?"

Miguel nodded and smiled. "Take all the time you need, sir. I wait for you outside." The visitor smiled again and turned, slowly walking to the black SUV parked on the street.

Luke closed the door and joined Meredith in the kitchen as she read the invitation. He didn't speak, knowing that he had to give his wife time to digest everything. Taking out his phone, Luke began searching for Stanton Yachts.

"Are you serious, babe? Is this legit?" Meredith said as she set the shiny golden envelope on the counter. Still holding its contents in her hand, she continued, "Who are these people? What kind of contest is this?"

"I don't know! Crazy, right?" Luke said as he continued his internet search. "Stanton Yachts bought some of our patents before we closed. They know our story, but I...well, I've never heard of any contest like this. I'm trying to find more information about them."

Meredith looked down at the invitation again. Shaking her head, she now read it out loud for her husband to hear.

Dear Mr. Voightmann,

Our team at Stanton Enterprises cordially invites you to attend a very special, week-long contest of entrepreneurs. On this guided first-class adventure, you'll travel across the Americas to meet some of the greatest entrepreneurial minds. You'll be challenged by your hosts to see if you're the ultimate entrepreneur. Do you have what it takes to win it all? The grand prize for this contest is valued at over ten million dollars.

We understand that this might seem like an unusual invitation and an unusual contest. To show our commitment and desire for you to join us, we've enclosed a certified check for one million dollars. If you decide to participate, please consider this a payment for your time and a down payment should you win. In the event you aren't selected as the winner, you'll still be entitled to the enclosed funds, as they represent the minimum guaranteed participation prize.

Please inform Mr. Chapman of your decision by Friday, May 24th at 6 p.m. He will also provide you with all the details and required paperwork to get started. We look forward to hearing from you and having you join us!

Warmly,

Stanton Enterprises

Meredith couldn't hold back any longer. Opening the folded piece of paper again, she said, "Honey, this is a million dollars."

"I know, babe. I know," Luke said calmly as he continued to research the company on his phone. "I don't know if this is some sick joke or what. Stanton Yachts are big-time players, but I can't imagine them spending money like this on some contest. Hold on for a second. I'm still reading."

Meredith held the certified check above her head to inspect it in the light. Ignoring her husband's request, she continued brainstorming out loud as if to solve a riddle. "Yep. It's real all right. Did you see it said ten million if you win? Maybe they're planning on putting everything on TV or something like that."

"I don't know, but I'm going to sort this out. I'll be back in a few minutes."

Luke's skeptical tone caused his wife to challenge him softly. "Go easy, Luke Voightmann. You're in CEO mode now. Just hear him out. Okay?"

"Oh, I'll hear him out all right. But if this joker is wasting our time with some stupid scam or if this is something to do with JROB Holdings, I'm taking him down, and he isn't leaving until the police show up," Luke threatened, partially joking, but ready for a brawl if needed.

After collecting the invitation and the check, he headed for the door. The visitor stood by the mailbox, leaning against the large SUV. Luke approached confidently, ready to get his questions answered. Miguel met him halfway and said, "Mr. Luke, what do you think about check? Now you know we are serious, right? What does your wife think? This is a big opportunity for you...yes?"

Luke took a breath and responded, "Actually, I don't know what to think about all of this, but I do have some questions."

Miguel continued smiling and answered, "I am happy to help you, sir. What do you want to know?"

As Miguel spoke, Luke noticed his visitor's watch—a gold Rolex Yacht-Master edition. Realizing the value of such an expensive watch and considering the man's appearance, Luke decided to weigh Miguel's words more carefully.

"So, why me? Do they really know who I am?" Luke said firmly, wondering if the contest holder knew the gritty details of his past.

Miguel smiled again and answered, "Yes, Mr. Luke, we know about you. Our team says you are a very bright entrepreneur who fall on hard times. They find you when you sell us boat designs. Everyone is very impressed with you. You have great ideas and dream big, Mr. Luke. You may have a hard time with Washington and news people, but we think you are a good fit for our contest."

Luke, still trying to comprehend the invitation, pushed further to understand everything. Opening the envelope and pulling out the check, he said, "So, just to be clear, there is a contest next week. If I win, I get $10 million. If I lose, I get to keep this check?"

"Yes, sir. You sign our contract tonight and take check to your bank tomorrow if you like. Sunday night, we fly on a private plane and meet hosts. You have a very good time, sir—good food too. I'll be with you on trip as your guide. I serve you and make sure you have everything you need. Nice hotel rooms and a big adventure."

Miguel's sincerity and excitement for the contest radiated from his smiling face. As unlikely as the invitation might have seemed, Luke couldn't help but start to believe what his visitor was saying.

"Well, I'm going to need more details. What contract? Where are we going? Who am I meeting? How many contestants are there?" Luke machine-gunned his questions, thoroughly trying to measure the legitimacy of the opportunity.

"Wait," Miguel responded. "I have our contract for you in car. I get it for you. You wait for one minute." Walking over to the SUV and reaching into the passenger side window, Miguel revealed a manila folder. Still smiling, he quickly walked back to Luke and handed it to him as he addressed his other questions.

"We leave Sunday at 7:00 p.m. I will pick you up. You need only clothes for sleeping and your passport. No money or anything else needed. I get your sizes tonight and bring you special clothes for adventure. We go on a private plane for the contest and you meet everyone. They all are very nice, and you like them very much. This time, we have four contestants in total, so the chances to win are very good. Then you have a big opportunity to make even more money. If you lose, you still keep your check and have lots of good memories. What more questions you have for me, Mr. Luke?"

Luke didn't respond. Instead, he focused on the contents of the folder. Taking two steps back, Luke quickly skimmed through the four-page contract, prefilled with his name, address, and already signed by a representative from Stanton Enterprises. Whoever these people were, they seemed to know Luke by name, and for whatever reason, they wanted him to join their contest. The certified check, the visitor's words, and the contract convinced Luke that the contest was credible. But credible or not, what Luke needed was more time to process everything.

"Sir, this is a lot to take in. Is it possible that you could give me a little more time? I just need a few more minutes to look through everything and talk with my wife. Would that be okay?" Luke said sincerely as he continued looking through the contract.

"Yes! Very good, Mr. Luke," Miguel said, delighted that Luke was considering the contest. "You take more time and think about it. Call me with any questions. But I need to hold check until you sign our contract. I come back later tonight to get everything from you and give you back check. Maybe at eight o'clock? Would this be okay with you, sir?"

Closing the folder, Luke nodded and handed Miguel the check. "That's perfect," he confirmed, shaking Miguel's hand firmly.

As his visitor drove away, Luke waved and plodded back to his door. Instead of entering, he hesitated, turning to sit down on the steps. He wasn't ready to go inside, at least not yet. He needed time to process everything and to wrestle with his thoughts. In all of his years, he couldn't remember a more absurd day. It all started that dreadful moment he woke up, smashing his head against the top bunk. The lawsuit from JROB Holdings initiated the pain, but it was traveling through his past that wrecked him. He missed his company. He missed his friend. More than anything, he missed his family. If those wounds weren't deep enough, the telephone call from his attorney brought a whole new level of torment. Would JROB Holdings really try to incriminate him?

Again, the heaviness of his situation started to grip him. Resting his elbows on his knees and running his fingers through his hair, he stared down at the ground. Sighing and bowing his head even lower, he caught a glimpse of the photo in his front shirt pocket. He'd forgotten he put it there to show Meredith and the boys. Now pulling the picture out again and lifting his head, he could see Dellin's silly smile. Just as before, the picture touched Luke's heart. As if Dellin were sitting on the step next to him, Luke began to speak out loud to his friend as he looked deeply into the picture.

"You know, I miss you, bro. I'm still upset at you for dying, but I do miss you and all the good times we had. You're in a better place and all, but it just sucks sometimes because I wish you were here with me. I'm all right, I guess, but life just isn't the same without you. Actually, who am I kidding? You know I'm a mess. Sometimes, I just don't know what to do. I wish you were still here. I'm sure we could have figured this out together. Even if we lost the company, we could have started something else—maybe selling a new gadget or something. I don't know what I'm going to do, bro. It's just—"

Hearing Luke's voice outside the door, Meredith quietly opened it to find him sitting on the steps.

"You okay?" she said softly.

Nodding his head, Luke responded without looking as he returned the picture to his pocket. "I'm okay. Can you give me a few minutes? I'll be in soon. I just need a little time to think."

Knowing the complexity of Luke's mind, she left him to his thoughts, well aware he'd return when he was ready to talk.

As the door closed, Luke turned his mind to the visitor, the contest, and the million-dollar check. Of all the oddities of the day, this one made the least amount of sense. Two years ago, he might have snubbed his nose at a contest like this. He probably would have demanded to know more details about the media coverage, other contestants' qualifications, and the $10-million prize money. Today was different. Luke was different. It wasn't the accolades or the money. What Luke cared about and desperately needed was something to get him unstuck. Besides, what could he do with the participation money anyway? Even if he won the contest, which Luke believed to be highly unlikely, he still wouldn't have enough to pay off his investors. Any prize money would either be used for the legal expense to fight JROB Holdings or handed over to them with his house and all his other assets. Either way, in light of his situation, the money really wouldn't make a difference.

Back and forth, his mind paced, skewed by the various scenarios, his emotions, and perhaps the side effects of his anxiety medication. Inwardly, he couldn't help but entertain the thoughts of joining the contest. Maybe it would be interesting, and a change of scenery might do him some good. At least it would be a distraction from his troubles. Before he could wrap his mind around accepting the invitation, his insecurities crept back in, and he assured himself he'd be outmatched by the others. Like a contestant on a reality TV show, Luke pictured himself saying something stupid, being embarrassed, and sent home on the very first day. Unsure if he could handle another disappointment, he reasoned the contest was likely a bad idea. Besides, he'd been on his boat for the last three nights, and his family missed him. With the afternoon sun starting to duck behind the trees, Luke looked at his watch. Shaking his head, he realized he had just a couple of hours until the visitor returned.

Standing up, a thought came to him that finally made sense. For all of his life, Luke seemed to always know exactly what he wanted. He made decisions quickly and lived with whatever happened. Like a strategic game of chess, Luke had maneuvered his way through life, moving pieces along to get what he wanted, whenever he wanted it. However, his decisions often affected others, especially those closest to him. Resolving the decision to join the contest wouldn't be his to make, Luke headed inside to talk with his wife.

5 MORE THAN A PLANE RIDE

The 13-mile ride to Kendall-Tamiami Executive Airport was quiet and uneventful. Resting his head back on the leather seat, Luke took a deep breath and closed his eyes, remembering the kind words Meredith had spoken before he left. "Our story isn't over, babe. You're only thirty-seven years old and have a lot of life to live. I'll call Doc on Monday and let him know you need to delay your meeting. He'll understand. I'll tell him you're going out of town and will be thinking it over. We'll figure out what to do when you get back. Besides, I think being around some other entrepreneurs might be good for you." He knew Meredith was right—he'd been in a funk for so long now.

In a matter of minutes, the black SUV pulled into a gravel parking lot on the south side of the airport. Luke noticed a fairly small twin-engine prop plane taxiing on the runway. *Is this our ride?* he thought. As the SUV parked, a man wearing a sweatshirt and baseball cap greeted Luke's driver. After exchanging pleasantries in Spanish, Miguel handed him the keys. Without saying a word to Luke, Miguel headed to the back of the SUV and began to unload the men's luggage. Luke followed, and after a short walk, the two men reached the tarmac.

Any concern Luke had about being uncomfortable instantly vanished as they approached the hundred-foot-long corporate jet. To Luke's delight, they wouldn't be traveling on a small propeller plane. Instead, it would be an indulgent trip on a Gulfstream 650ER. Proudly displaying the words "Stanton Enterprises" on its side, the black aircraft stood ready for its passengers. Luke's smile wouldn't allow him to hide his excitement. He loved this jet and had always dreamed about riding in one. He had traveled on private jets a few times before, but none were like this. The Gulfstream 650ER was only within reach of large corporations and billionaires. With a maximum cruising speed of nearly the speed of sound, the plane could go from Miami to New York in about two hours. If distance was the aim, it could carry nineteen passengers from New York to Hong Kong without stopping for fuel. With a long waiting list to purchase one and a price tag of nearly $70 million, Luke often joked that his biggest mistake was forgoing aviation and getting into yacht building.

Seeing Luke's face, Miguel said, "You like plane, sir? You haven't traveled like this before, huh?"

Miguel didn't give Luke a chance to respond and swiftly lifted all the luggage into the exterior storage hatch that was left open. Then he turned and headed for the plane's door.

"I've been on corporate jets before," Luke offered in a response that was ignored. Miguel, seeming to be on a mission, hurried up the stairs as he shouted a few words in Spanish to announce they had arrived. Luke followed him onboard. Again, Miguel shouted something in Spanish. No response. After a quick look into the cockpit, Miguel proceeded hastily down the center aisle. The two seats for the pilots lay empty, but Luke didn't care about the cockpit. He wanted to see the luxury. As he continued following Miguel down the center aisle, Luke passed by a large reclining chair, shiny table, and small television screen, which he assumed was for Stanton's crew. Passing by the forward lavatory, they entered the galley. Pristine granite countertops, wood grain cabinets, and high-end stainless steel completed the area. The smell of fresh leather and ionized air made him pause as he inspected the forward cabin that included a set of four immaculate chairs divided by the center aisle. Retractable tables made of polished wood adorned the walls beneath the large picture windows.

"It's like a CataSail Yacht in the sky! I can handle this for a week," Luke laughed to himself as he approached midpoint on the plane.

Reaching the third living space, Miguel stopped and waited for Luke to catch up. "Sit where you like, Mr. Luke. We'll take two flights tonight. We go to Dallas to get AJ on first leg of our trip—and then start your journey. You get lots of rest, sir. We have a very busy day tomorrow."

Again, Miguel didn't wait for an answer as he continued towards the rear of the plane. Pulling his phone up to his ear, he was instantly on a call and intensely speaking in Spanish. Whoever he was calling seemed to be in trouble. Changing directions now, Miguel headed to the front of the plane and then down the stairs as he continued the phone call. Luke had only been with the man a short while but had already decided that he liked him immensely. It was hard not to like someone who was clearly focused on the job at hand but also smiling as they worked. Though Miguel spoke with a slight accent and often omitted certain words, he was easy to understand and extremely polite. However, what Luke appreciated most about him was his efficiency and the pace at which he moved. Perhaps Miguel had a tough boss, or maybe the plane was running late. Regardless, Miguel seemed to be on a mission to get the trip on schedule.

Too excited to sit down just yet, Luke continued his discovery. Looking to the rear of the plane, he admired the five-foot-long credenza with a flatscreen television mounted on top. It seemed to be strategically positioned across from the four chairs and table used for dining and in-air conference meetings. Beyond the conference table, he could see a leather couch partially blocked by the privacy of a polished wall. Already familiar with the aircraft's layout, Luke concluded that it was Stanton's private quarters. Before Luke could finish his inspection, he heard the sound of men speaking in Spanish behind him. Miguel, followed by two men dressed in solid black suits, boarded the plane and passed through the galley. Luke smiled and waved to greet them.

"Mr. Luke, please meet our pilots—Mr. Severino and Mr. Sanchez. They are very experienced pilots. They take good care of us while we fly this week." Miguel's introduction and desire to make Luke feel safe was endearing, and Luke extended his hand to exchange introductions.

As the pilots returned to the cockpit, Luke sat down at a window seat. Miguel headed for the galley and began pressing buttons on the console. With doors now shut and engines turning, the main cabin's lights dimmed as multiple chimes indicated the cabin was being pressurized and made ready. Once complete, Miguel sat down in the forward cabin chair, opened up a journal, and began writing. Three minutes later, the plane taxied to the runway, and within five minutes, they reached two thousand feet. Luke briefly peeked out the window, revealing the skyline and sparkling waters of his home city. The sun was now below the horizon but still offered plenty of light everywhere the eye could see.

It didn't take long for Miguel to be up and about. "Mr. Luke, we eat after Dallas stop. Would you like a snack or drink while you wait?"

Relieved he would be waited on, Luke responded, "I ate a little something with my family a while ago, but what do you have to drink, my man?"

Miguel, eager to serve his new guest, smiled and said, "I can provide water, coffee, tea, red or white wine. We have Coca-Cola products as well. In Dallas, we receive a new stock with more options. What can I get for you, Mr. Luke?"

Though something stronger might have calmed his nerves, Luke asked for a glass of red wine and thanked Miguel for his service. Almost instantly, Miguel returned with a freshly opened bottle and wine glass.

"Would you like a taste, sir?" Miguel offered as he popped the cork and began pouring a small amount into the glass.

"I'm sure it is fine. You can fill 'er up, if that's okay," Luke quickly responded, showing he was no wine snob. "I don't know if you have a minute to spare, but I was hoping you could tell me more about the contest. We didn't get much time at my house on Friday, and I'd like to learn a little more. You also mentioned we're picking up someone named AJ. Can you tell me more about him?"

Miguel nodded as he placed the cork back into the bottle and proceeded to sit across from Luke. "I can try to help, sir, but I don't have all details yet. Tonight, I will find out more about our schedule after I speak with AJ. I know we are headed to Peru tomorrow, but I don't know about other days yet. Our contest is very easy though. You fly to meet hosts. I introduce you to them, and they ask you questions. You have a very big adventure all week. And Mr. AJ, he is a very nice man and in charge of contest. I'm sure you'll do very well this week because we look for people with a good business spirit—like you, Mr. Luke."

"Thank you, Miguel. I'm sure everything will be fine. Did you say that we're meeting AJ and then headed to Peru? Are you talking about Peru, like the country in South America?" Luke said to further clarify.

"Yes. As I said, it is a big adventure. After Dallas stop, we'll head to Peru and you will start contest tomorrow morning. AJ and I will be your guides this week and take you to meet hosts."

Luke's personality typically caused him to analyze every detail. His wheels would often spin for hours, with his mind quickly moving through multiple scenarios. Had he still been a CEO, he might have drilled for more details, but not today. He didn't really care where he was going or who he was meeting. For him, this was a chance to get away from everything.

"You've been very helpful, my friend. I appreciate the time you spent with me to answer my questions. I'm sure we'll figure it all out as we go. Thank you again," Luke said and then took a sip from his glass.

Miguel smiled, stood up, and disappeared to the forward cabin. Within twenty minutes, Luke finished his wine. Pressing the recline button on his seat, the footrest extended, and the soft leather chair pushed backward. Deciding to relax, he closed his eyes, not thinking of anything in particular.

A small patch of turbulence jolted Luke's head forward, causing him to wake up from his nap. As he reached for the button to return his chair, he could tell they were descending. The empty wine glass and bottle had been removed, and a small blanket now covered him. Looking at his watch, he was surprised to see he had slept for nearly forty minutes. More surprising was the fact the plane was already descending on Dallas. Luke yawned and rubbed his eyes, trying to prepare himself for whatever was coming next. After taking a deep breath, he folded the blanket and placed it on the chair across from him.

Noticing Luke was awake, Miguel appeared next to him to gather the blanket. Speaking enthusiastically, he said, "You all set for landing, Mr. Luke? I think wine made you a little sleepy. I covered you up so you get plenty of rest."

"Yes, my friend," Luke responded. "It has been a very long day for me, and I didn't sleep well last night. Thank you for the blanket and hospitality."

Within fifteen minutes, the plane touched down softly at a small airport just outside of downtown Dallas. What occurred next took Luke by surprise. Looking down the center aisle through the galley, he saw all three men crowded together while Miguel made the adjustments to open the cabin door. The men's Spanish conversation became louder and louder as a wave of excitement seemed to come over them. The copilot, Sanchez, then burst out in a loud Spanish song, and laughter broke out amongst the men. Though the scene lasted less than a minute, this professional crew had turned into a bunch of juveniles as they awaited their new passenger.

Outside of his window, Luke could see that Miguel had exited the plane and was walking towards a vehicle that slowly rolled to a stop. Bright headlights stung Luke's eyes through the darkness as he tried to make out the passenger now approaching the plane. Deciding it was a lost effort, Luke closed his window and took a deep breath. His anxiety continued to grow as a cold sweat started to form on his forehead. Taking another deep breath, Luke closed his eyes to focus. For the first time in ten months, he'd be forced to talk business and face his own insecurities—and today, he'd have to do it without his anxiety medication. Still sitting in the medicine cabinet at home, the little white pills wouldn't be making the trip with him. The truth is, Luke was glad. The prescribed medication didn't help much anyway, and Luke wanted his mind to be as sharp as possible for the contest.

Before Luke could fully relax, Spanish words again broke out from the front of the plane. This time, the voice was different from the others. It was firm but spoke much slower. The words came from a short white man who boarded the plane. With his back turned to Luke, the man proceeded to shake hands with the pilots who stood in the cockpit to be greeted. Miguel followed behind, carrying several bags. Another boisterous celebration followed with all four men laughing and speaking in Spanish together. If that wasn't enough for Luke to feel out of place, the new passenger now began to sing out loud. Though off-key—and quite terrible—the four men erupted in laughter as they all joined in singing the song Luke had heard moments ago. Before the celebration got further out of hand, Miguel said something in Spanish, and all four men made eye contact with Luke, who looked away, pretending to fumble with his seatbelt.

Now turning to face Luke was the short, stocky man with pasty white skin, appearing to be in his mid-sixties. Luke could only assume this was AJ, his guide for the week. Wearing a gray tucked-in flannel shirt, blue jeans, and cowboy boots, the man smiled and nodded at Luke. Holding up one finger, as if to say, "I'll be right there," the man continued speaking a few more words.

As he turned to start down the aisle, Luke stood up to greet him, noticing the man's large golden belt buckle, almost as big as the state of Texas. The man looked the part of a cleaned-up cowboy who had just left the farm for a night on the town—minus the hat. His neatly parted gray hair and clean-shaven face reflected what Luke thought to be an idyllic cattle rancher.

"Luke, I presume," the man said with a country drawl as he stretched his hand out to Luke's. "I'm AJ. It's a pleasure to meet you, sir. So glad you could join us on our little adventure this week."

"Nice to meet you too. I'm looking forward to it," Luke said while firmly squeezing AJ's hand in response.

"Sit down, sit down, let's get started right away. I know you've already had one flight, but can I get you anything before we get talking?"

"No thanks! I'm good, sir."

AJ held up a hand to get Miguel's attention and then continued speaking to Luke. "So, we actually know a whole lot about you already, but not much about your family and what you've been up to over the last few months."

"Yeah, I guess just about everybody knows who I am. So, you probably know that you guys purchased some of our assets before we closed shop. I don't know what you want to hear, but it's been a hard year for us—the family is good though. I have a great wife, Meredith. We've been married for ten years and have two little boys, Pauly and David." Luke's nerves caused him to speak faster than usual and he was relieved when Miguel appeared again, allowing him to cut his response short.

"Miguel, could you get me a Diet Coke, please? Are you sure I can't get you anything, Luke?" AJ said, making sure Luke was content.

"I'm good right now. Maybe a little later. Thanks though."

AJ continued, "We all followed your story for a long time, and I'm sorry you had to go through all that. Anyway, I'm guessing you're interested in why we've brought you here?"

Luke nodded, curious about the man's words and the contest.

"I'll get right to it then. We're holding this contest to locate a high-level leader for our organization. Now, before I move on, I hope you know that we take this contest seriously. Win or lose, we'll drop you off next Sunday and you can keep that check. If you win—well, that's a whole different animal. I know you've been a CEO and ran your own show, so you might not be looking for anything just yet, but I hope you'll at least consider it."

AJ paused as Miguel returned with an ice-filled glass, fizzing with his favorite beverage. Taking a sip, AJ intentionally waited, giving Luke a chance to gather his thoughts.

"Well, I'll be honest with you since you've made your intentions clear. Regarding accepting a position with your company, I don't know about that. I haven't really thought about it. I don't know what Stanton pays you to hold these contests, but a million dollars doesn't go as far as it used to. To be honest, I came because I was curious...and well, my wife thought it would be good for me. Stanton seems like he runs a great business—and I'm sure he treats you all well—but I'll probably end up starting another company one day."

A smile slowly crept across AJ's face as he lifted his hand once again to get Miguel's attention. Almost as if he'd been told the same thing by other CEOs, he seemed to be unfazed and amused by Luke's unwillingness to be coerced.

"Actually, would you excuse me a minute, Luke? I'm sorry to cut you off," he said politely. "I just remembered I need to tell Miguel about something, and if I don't tell him right now, I'll forget. Don't lose your thought, my boy. I'll be right back." AJ moved forward until he reached Miguel, who was preparing something in the galley. Taking him by the arm, AJ began whispering in his ear. Whatever he was saying didn't seem too important, and within a couple of minutes, he returned to his seat as the plane began slowly rolling forward.

AJ fastened his seatbelt as he said, "Luke, I'm so sorry about that. At my age, I've got to say what I'm thinking before I forget. Please pardon me for interrupting you. You were saying, sir?"

"Well, I guess I was saying that I probably wouldn't be interested because I'm going to start another company. Honestly, I can't imagine working for someone else after all these years. Besides, I haven't met the other contestants yet. What are their stories? And who's to say I'd win anyway?" Luke's tone changed slightly as the weight of his past brought out his insecurity.

Undeterred by Luke's words, AJ continued to speak as the plane lifted off the runway. "Well, we got a long way to go. Why don't we just see what happens? Unfortunately, you won't be meeting any of the other contestants. That's not how this works. There are four of you competing in our contest. A couple played along last week, and I've got you and one other young lady this week, so let's see how everything plays out."

Luke tried to wrap his mind around AJ's words. *Why won't I be meeting any of the other contestants?* And then it dawned on him that this wasn't really a contest after all. For all legal purposes, they might be calling it a contest, but this was nothing more than strategic executive headhunting. The million-dollar participation prize money was literally a bribe to get people to come on the interview. Oddly enough, Luke didn't care. He'd already deposited the check and was now even more intrigued by their unique hiring strategy.

"Plays out? I'm not sure I understand, sir," Luke said with a smile, now wondering if he could pry into AJ's plan. "From what you're saying, this doesn't sound like a contest. It sounds more like recruiting. You're paying me to interview for a job when I don't know anything about the position. I appreciate the money and all, but how do you know I'd even be interested?"

AJ leaned forward as he responded with a chuckle. "Well, you're right—I don't know if you'd be interested or not—but you're going to find that we do things differently around here. Let me start by saying that most people have never heard about us—that is, Stanton Enterprises. We are the mother ship. We fly under the radar and kind of like it that way. What you don't know is that we're a multibillion-dollar organization that includes thirty-two privately held corporations. Our assets include clothing brands, marinas, banks, beverage manufacturers, breweries, internet and technology products, real estate companies, and a bunch of other industries I could rattle off. Obviously, you've heard of Stanton Yachts, who purchased some of your assets. Well, that's the tip of the iceberg, my boy. There are thirty-one other companies besides that one, many of them you've heard about."

Luke was immediately intrigued by AJ's words, confidence, and posture. The thought of a billion-dollar business piqued Luke's interest as he continued his questioning. "Well, that sounds impressive. So, it's a big conglomerate then? But what does that have to do with me?"

AJ didn't flinch. "It isn't any conglomerate like you've seen, that's for sure. We keep the entities completely separate, and they are all privately held corporations. They each have separate boards, separate books, their own assets, and most importantly, their own leadership teams. We don't typically acquire companies and don't participate in mergers unless one of our founders is ready to exit. You see, we launch companies from scratch and build them from the ground up. You've been invited to the contest because we're looking for entrepreneurial talent." As he finished speaking, he looked out the window and sipped the final drops of his Diet Coke. AJ seemed to be deeply comfortable sharing about the business model and contest, and Luke could tell that he was an intelligent man.

"What role am I being considered for? Which company? Is Stanton looking for someone to take over the yacht business? The model sounds interesting, but I'm not sure Wall Street would agree that keeping everything separate is the best use of your resources. It seems like centralizing some assets might save a lot of money." Luke had intended for his comment to make him sound knowledgeable about business. Instead, his words came out more arrogant than he would have liked.

As the plane started to level off, AJ placed his glass in the cup holder and continued. "Well, Wall Street might not like it, but we don't care. Our philosophy and values are different. Besides, our returns are better than the market, and we've got a waiting list of private money ready to invest. Of course, we could play their game. We could buy companies at the height of the market and pay top dollar, but that's not our model. Our secret sauce is identifying the right leadership and allowing them room for the exponential growth they can create for our organizations. You see, our CEOs build the business and we just finance them."

"Excuse me, sir, but I will have your food ready shortly. Would you like to eat here or at dining table tonight?" Miguel said quietly, interrupting the conversation.

Without verbally responding to Miguel, AJ pointed to the dining table and then stood up, continuing the conversation with Luke. "You're not here for Stanton Yachts. This would be for something else. It's for a CEO position with high stakes and big rewards. We'll get to that if you win, my boy, but we got a long way to go yet. I'm going to wash up in the front. You can use the restroom back there if you'd like." Without another word, AJ turned and headed to the front of the plane.

Luke's passage through the luxury aft suite didn't take long. Opening the door to the ensuite lavatory, he noticed the glass shower, wardrobe, and embroidered cotton towels. His curiosity now overflowed as he scrubbed his hands for nearly a minute, trying to understand the contest. *Why did they invite me? Don't they know my story?* Though Luke was now deeply intrigued by the contest and why they were interested in him, he couldn't allow his emotions to engage, at least not until he understood more.

By the time the men had returned to the table, Miguel had everything prepared. A linen tablecloth, silverware, ice water, and two wine glasses were precisely placed as if they were dining at a five-star restaurant. Without asking for permission, Miguel poured two glasses of chardonnay and then disappeared back to the galley. Within seconds, he returned with the men's entrées—barbecue chicken, mashed potatoes, and cornbread. AJ thanked Miguel for his service and then continued speaking to Luke.

"I hope you like barbecue. This is some good ol' boy chicken."

AJ didn't bother with his silverware and unashamedly grabbed the drumstick from his plate, taking a huge bite. Luke couldn't help but feel at home as he looked up and saw a small dab of barbecue sauce on AJ's chin. Grabbing his own piece of chicken, he dug in with the same passion. As they continued eating, Luke found another question that he thought appropriate. "So, tell me more about this contest. Is this normal for Stanton? You guys hold these often?"

"Whenever we're trying to fill a CEO role, we hold contests due to the high stakes. It might sound bizarre to some, but we'll do just about everything we can to get the right person on top, even paying them a million dollars. There is a strict hiring process for all of our department leaders and managers too, but we don't hold contests for those roles, and they don't get to fly around in a corporate jet. As I said, we do things differently, but all hiring of our key leadership positions is based upon one and the same thing."

Now curious to understand what triggers a hire, Luke pressed in, trying to get clarity from AJ. "The same thing? Are we talking MBA, experience, or what? It makes sense—"

AJ interrupted, "Regarding what we look for...we call it, the *EntreSpirit*. Over the next few days, you're going to meet our hosts. All of them have very sharp entrepreneurial minds, and they're going to ask you some questions and teach you a little bit about the *EntreSpirit*."

As he finished, AJ took a sip of wine and wiped his mouth with the napkin from his lap. Luke took a bite of mashed potatoes as he pondered AJ's words. He was curious and said, "Did you say *EntreSpirit*? I've never heard that word before. Honestly, I have no idea what that is."

AJ responded, covering his full mouth with a napkin. "Yes, *EntreSpirit*." After swallowing his food, he continued. "It's made up of our five principles of entrepreneurship, and it's what we look for in our winners. You're going to learn all about it this week. I don't know if you've got it or not. I'm just here to take you on the trip, but the hosts you meet this week will ask you the questions. They'll be able to tell if you have the *EntreSpirit*. I wouldn't worry about it anyway, my boy. As you said, you probably wouldn't take a position, so just have fun and enjoy yourself. Besides, we've got all week to discuss everything."

It was easy for Luke to like AJ. He was confident and smart but not pretentious. His country accent and casual language made Luke feel comfortable, like he'd known him for years. Though some twenty-five years his senior, Luke felt a connection with him and was glad that AJ and Miguel were his guides for the week.

As the men finished their conversation, the table was cleared. AJ insisted Luke sleep in the private suite in the rear of the plane. Though Luke politely objected, AJ remained firm, as he was certain Luke would need the quality rest. Besides, AJ wanted to discuss the week's details with Miguel. Reluctantly, Luke accepted and headed to the suite which

Miguel had set up with fresh linens. Inwardly, Luke was ecstatic for the opportunity to have Stanton's suite, and with a touch of a button, the automatic door closed. As Luke laid down that night, some 49,000 feet in the air, he had no idea where he was going or what he was doing. Intrigued by the situation, he intended to think through AJ's words before going to sleep. But he couldn't fight how tired he was, and as he closed his eyes, he nodded off.

6 A MISSION IN THE AMAZON

As the plane touched down, the runway shook Luke's cabin, startling him awake from his nightmare and causing him to gasp out loud. The dream had followed him again, replaying the tragic accident in his sleep. Sitting up, Luke read the LED clock on the wall, telling him it was 4:54 in the morning. After taking a deep breath, he collapsed back onto his pillow and began wiping the cold sweat from his forehead. A wave of nausea followed, causing him to cough profusely. When the plane finally rolled to a stop, he stepped into the attached bathroom to wash his face and get something to drink.

"You've got to pull yourself together, Luke Voightmann!" he said to himself in the mirror as he dried his face with a towel. After downing a full glass of water, his coughing subsided, and he laid back down. Luke desperately wanted the day to start, but it didn't. Just like his life, the plane and his future stood motionless in the dark, waiting for daybreak. Though he tried to think about the contest, his exhaustion was too much, and he drifted back to sleep.

Knock, knock. "Mr. Luke! Good morning. I have clothes for you, sir," Miguel said softly, hoping to wake his guest but not scare him.

"Thank you, Miguel. I'll be right out," Luke acknowledged as he opened his eyes. The morning sun now streaked through the half-open window, and he was surprised to see an hour and a half had passed. Opening his window all the way, he could now see a cluster of lush palm trees planted at the corner of a building. The landscape looked like his hometown of Miami—including all the signs in Spanish.

After using the bathroom and freshening up, Luke opened the cabin door, still dressed in his T-shirt and sleep pants. Miguel sat at the dining table. Seeing Luke, he quickly put down his coffee cup and approached his guest.

"Did you sleep well, Mr. Luke?" he asked sincerely.

"Yes. Thank you," Luke responded with a smile.

"Very good, sir," Miguel said as he handed Luke the zipped garment bag. "Here are your clothes for today. Please let me know if everything fits okay. I'll get your breakfast ready while you change."

As promised, Miguel provided clothing for the contest, and his measurements were spot on. Though the clothes weren't something Luke would normally wear, at least they fit. Starting with a pair of lightweight khaki pants and continuing with a white long sleeve cotton shirt, he quickly dressed. Completing his outfit was a pair of black rubber boots that stretched up to his knees. Luke could only wonder where he could be going to need such an outrageous outfit. Shoving his cell phone, passport, and wallet in his pocket, he headed back out to start his day.

At the table, Miguel had prepared a cup of coffee, orange juice, and a plate of bacon, eggs, and toast. As Luke sat down, Miguel again appeared from the galley, dressed in an identical outfit. Smiling, he said, "We will be twins today, Mr. Luke. Go ahead and eat without me as I already ate a little while ago."

Luke returned Miguel's smile and started eating a piece of toast as Miguel headed to the front of the plane. Though unsure of the plan for the day, one thing was certain—AJ was nowhere to be found. Eating in silence, Luke thought about the oddity of his situation. *Why am I in Peru? Who am I meeting? And where is AJ?* His mental struggle continued as he wondered why he'd even been chosen for the contest. Within ten minutes, he'd barely touched his breakfast when Miguel returned and said, "Is your food okay, sir? You didn't eat much."

"Oh, I'm sorry Miguel. It was great. I guess I don't have much of an appetite this morning."

"Don't worry, sir. You'll be very hungry tonight after today's big adventure. Okay, let's get going then. You ready to go?" Miguel said with a big smile as he picked up Luke's plate.

"I'm ready. Any hint on where we're headed?" Luke asked as he stood up to follow.

"We are in the city of Iquitos," Miguel responded. "You been here before, sir?"

"Iquitos, huh? Nope—I've never heard of it."

Miguel didn't respond. Instead, he just smiled as he completed his chores, quickly discarding Luke's leftovers and placing the dirty dish in the sink. After passing the empty cockpit, the men continued down the stairs. Inside the airport, they were directed to Peruvian customs. Thankfully, Miguel interpreted, and in a matter of minutes, both men were cleared with their passports stamped. Exiting through a set of glass doors, a bright white helicopter greeted them, quietly sitting on its pad. The pilot stood by, calmly waiting for his passengers, and leaning against the machine as if it were an old friend. Seeing Luke and Miguel, he jumped into action, quickly opening the doors to prepare for takeoff.

With seatbelts fastened and headsets secured over their ears, a slow whooshing sound began as the pilot started the engine. The blades spun faster and faster until they reached a steady hum. In an instant, the helicopter climbed into the morning sky with its adrenaline-filled passengers. Luke wasn't yet prepared for the majesty awaiting him. Just ahead, the lush green vegetation encompassed everything. Flying two hundred feet off the ground, they quickly reached the dense forest, and he beheld the glory of the jungle. Before long, he spotted a wide river with brown sandy waters, dividing the jungle and flowing freely.

Miguel tapped Luke's leg and spoke through the headset. "There—Amazon River!"

Luke nodded, not fully comprehending Miguel's words. When it hit him, Luke's excitement exploded, and he said, "Seriously? That's the Amazon?"

Miguel laughed. "Like I told you, big adventure! We fly for one hour until we reach village. Today we head deep into jungle."

Exhilarated by the thought of being in the Amazon rainforest, Luke quickly returned to his window as the helicopter lowered to fifty feet above the bustling river. Below, long narrow speedboats roofed with blue tarps quickly taxied passengers. Shanty buildings on stilts covered with thatched roofs dotted the shore, some reaching into the water. Luke spotted two teenage boys net fishing on a boat who waved to him. Without hesitation, he smiled and quickly returned the gesture. He couldn't help but be mesmerized by the swollen river overtaking its banks.

For fifteen minutes, the helicopter continued its course, following the wide and powerful river. Just as Luke might have lost interest, the helicopter turned left towards the jungle, lifting high to clear the tree line. Increasing in speed and altitude, the forest below merged into a sea of green vegetation. Looking ahead, he could make out another river in the distance.

"What's that?" Luke said, pointing to the water.

"Rio Napo," Miguel answered. "That's path we take to see Mr. James. You enjoying flight, Mr. Luke? It's very beautiful, right?"

"I've never seen anything like it."

"We have nice weather here in morning, but bad storms come later today. Pilots can't fly then, so we will return by boat," Miguel commented as the helicopter descended over the river below.

Unlike the Amazon, the Napo River was narrower, twisting and winding through the jungle. It was also quieter, with very few motorboats or thatched huts. They continued following the river for another twenty minutes until they reached a small tributary, partially hidden by the dense jungle. The helicopter slowed, then gently lifted above the trees to follow the waterway below. Scoping the banks between the trees, not a single sign of human life could be found. Whoever Luke would meet today seemed to live deep in the jungle.

At a quarter past eight o'clock, they finally reached their destination. Rounding another bend, an opening in the trees revealed a wooden dock. Starting somewhere within the forest and ending fifteen feet over the water, it would be easy to miss if it didn't have a large orange flag marking its location. Familiar with the jungle, the pilot turned right and headed a few hundred yards inland toward an opening in the trees. As they landed, the pilot exited and opened his passengers' doors. With the engine still humming, Miguel yelled something in Spanish and handed the pilot a few bills in Peruvian currency. Within seconds, the helicopter vanished.

Again, Luke was unprepared. Now unhidden by the helicopter's roar, the sounds of the jungle came alive. Like a musical soundtrack for relaxation—birds and wild animals seemed to cry out in wild notes everywhere, and the rustling sounds of branches provided the natural percussion section. And then, just as Luke was getting lost in the native tune, a loud screech came from behind, causing him to jump.

"It's okay, Mr. Luke. Only some crazy monkeys who don't like helicopters. This way. I will take you to village now. We walk just a few minutes," Miguel said as he chuckled at Luke and began walking forward towards a trail.

As they started their trek, the humidity engulfed the jungle, causing both men to be drenched in sweat. Passing by large ancient trees draped with vines, the ground grew softer and softer until it covered their boots with dark red mud. Though Luke wanted to talk and learn more about where they were going, it was nearly impossible for him to engage Miguel—the brilliant sights and sounds of the forest simply wouldn't allow it.

Soon, they reached a large clearing, probably spanning three acres. Though protected by the shade of taller trees, the underbrush and scrubby trees had been removed. Standing in the clearing, Luke identified his destination—a village with a collection of buildings, all of which were elevated on stilts and connected by a maze of boardwalks. On the left stood several dozen circular huts with thatched roofs, each having a wooden rocking chair or bench outside. To Luke's right were four larger buildings with corrugated tin roofs. The center of the entire wooden settlement presented the largest building, rising two stories. A giant tree protruded through its center, stretching some two hundred feet to the top of the canopy. With multiple doorways, this thatched-roof building seemed to be the epicenter of the village. In front of the entire scene stood a wide series of stairs that served as a welcoming entrance to the lifted community.

Following Miguel upward, Luke noticed the dark brown boardwalks and freshly stained railings. At last, his location made sense. Through the forest, the water sparkled, and Luke could see the long dock and orange flag that connected the village to the river. Raised high off the ground, it was now clear that the lifted dwellings protected the people from certain floods. Luke shook his head, realizing he'd flown over the village just moments ago, but it remained hidden inside the dense forest.

Without hesitating, Miguel continued forward across the long wooden walkways, stopping periodically to greet a few elderly natives they passed along the way. Reaching the last hut, Miguel knocked, saying, "Mr. James! Are you ready for us, sir?"

"I'm here. Come on in, Miguel," a voice responded from inside.

After removing their muddy boots, the men quietly walked into the hut. As they reached the living room, Luke admired how well-built the structure was, with wooden plank walls and screen windows throughout. Furnished with a wicker couch and chair, the primary room was tastefully decorated. A small coffee table and rolltop desk completed the simple but comfortable design. Passing an opening as they walked, Luke could see that they used the other half of the hut as private living quarters.

Miguel seemed to feel comfortable in this place as he headed straight for the man, embracing him and greeting him in Spanish. They spoke for roughly a minute, and Luke assumed he was debriefing him.

"Mr. Luke, please meet your first host, Mr. James Montgomery," Miguel said as he introduced the two.

Standing just five foot seven, James Montgomery was a strong, stocky man, with a clean-shaven face, in his late fifties or early sixties. The man's pale white skin and gray wavy hair assured Luke that he wasn't native to this part of the world. He was casually dressed in blue jeans, a green polo shirt, and a pair of white tennis shoes. As Luke greeted his host, he noticed a scar roughly four inches long on his right cheek.

"Pleasure to meet you, Luke. Please call me James," the man said warmly with a strong country accent, likely originating from Alabama or Georgia. "Won't you have a seat, and we'll get started."

As the men sat down, James continued speaking. "Since I'm your first host, I'll try to tell you how this works. I'm sure AJ told you already, but it's our job to see if you're a good fit for us. Today, I'll be asking you a few questions, and I'll try to explain a little about the *EntreSpirit*. Keep in mind there are no right or wrong answers here. So, before we get started, do you have any questions for me?"

Truthfully, Luke had dozens of questions. To name one, he wanted to know what the man was doing in the middle of the jungle. Content that he'd figure everything out soon enough, he smiled and said, "I can't think of anything off the top of my head."

James nodded and pulled out a stack of white index cards. After quickly reviewing them, he began. "Okay, well, let's get started. My part of the contest is to figure out what makes you tick. Could you start by telling me why you started a sailboat company?"

Luke hesitated for a moment and thought through the question. "Well, it's kind of a blur. We're talking about fifteen years ago, but I'd say we started because we had a good idea. Back then, there wasn't as much technology in boats, and we felt like we could make a good product. The business kind of found us, I guess you could say."

"So, is boating a passion of yours or something you wanted to share with others?" James quickly added to clarify.

"Is my passion boating?" Luke said, echoing the question. "Not really. But Dellin, my business partner, loved boating. He's the one that grew up on the water."

"Hmmm…interesting." After pausing for a couple of seconds, James continued with another question. "So, if boating isn't your passion, can you share what some of your passions might be?"

Luke scratched his beard as he considered the question. "That's a tough one. I don't have too many things I'm passionate about. I used to say that CataSail was my passion—also my family."

"Okay. Anything else besides your company or family?" James clarified with a slightly emphatic tone.

Luke's struggle continued as he tried to communicate his thoughts. "Honestly, I can't think of anything. I've been so busy for such a long time, I don't really—"

Undeterred by Luke's response, James interrupted. "Let me see if I can explain this. I'm looking for what motivates you. In other words, I need to find out—"

"You mean like my vision?" Luke blurted out.

James shook his head and continued, "No. I'm not after your vision. Your vision is what you do. I'm looking for your why. Usually, it's found in one's hobbies, causes, and deeply rooted core values. For example, how do you spend your weekends? Do you volunteer for anything? Where do you invest your time and money?"

Feeling a little confined by the many questions and unsure of how to answer them, Luke leaned forward to address the question instead of answering it. "Correct me if I'm wrong, but it sounds like you're trying to see if I have any special causes that I care about."

"Well, not exactly, but do you?" James asked.

"I wish I could say that I volunteer down at the local soup kitchen in my spare time, but that's just not my life. It took a lot to run CataSail. Honestly, I didn't have time for any of that."

James nodded, saying, "I understand that leading your organization probably required a lot of your time. Let me help you understand what we're after here. I'm trying to understand your purpose in life, or what we like to call your mission. That's where I'm—"

"My mission?" Luke interrupted.

"Yes...your mission! We want to know if there is anything you deeply care about. I'm talking about a heartfelt passion, like a higher calling. Something you think about often, almost like a cause. Try to think about it for a minute—there's got to be something," James said directly, hoping for a reaction.

Unable to understand why it even mattered, Luke began to show a little frustration. After he took a deep breath, he responded. "With all due respect, sir, I really don't know what you want me to say. I...I don't support any special causes. I don't feed the hungry or give to the poor, and frankly, I don't care to do so. If they want money or food, they can get a job and work for it. I'm sorry if that sounds harsh, but it's just not me. Furthermore, I'm not interested in saving the whales, or for that matter, the rainforest either. I wish I had some hobbies, but I don't. I wish I could tell you that I've worked to make the world a better place, but I can't. I have lived the life of a busy entrepreneur. I get up, I go to work, and then I do the same thing again, day after day."

James shook his head and pressed the question further, seeming to be dissatisfied with Luke's words. This time, he raised his voice a little for emphasis. "I'm not buying it, young man. There has to be something! You're telling me there's NOTHING, and I mean absolutely nothing you're passionate about in life? I'm sorry, but I can't buy that!"

The host's words weren't necessarily rude, but they were direct, and Luke took them as an insult to his character. Trying to defend himself, Luke jabbed back. His tone wasn't close to a yell, but his words were bold. "Oh, I'm passionate about a lot of things. They're just not what you're looking for. But just so you know, I'm passionate about making money and enjoying the finer things in life! I'm passionate about my house on the water, going on vacation, and a glass of expensive wine. As you can tell, I love to eat. I'm passionate about filet mignon—cooked to perfection, and sushi too. Let's see, I love watching sports while enjoying a cold beer. Now, beer-drinking—that's another thing I'm passionate about, and one might even say I've become an expert at lately."

James beamed, and as Luke finished speaking, he laughed out loud, causing Miguel to join him and removing the tension in the room. "Well... all right! That's a great starting point," James said as he continued to laugh. To Luke's surprise, his host welcomed his response and authenticity. Miguel patted Luke on the back to encourage him. Though slightly embarrassed by his own words, Luke was glad that it softened the mood.

James continued, saying, "Let me explain a few things, and what I'm about to share might help you. You see, we believe that the *EntreSpirit* revolves around one's passions—and flowing in those passions. We want to know what you love and why you love it. I asked you about your passions because we believe it is critical for every entrepreneur to see his work as a personal mission. Does that make any sense?"

Now in a calmer tone, Luke responded. "I hear what you're saying, and it sounds good and all, but I think most people wake up every day motivated by one thing—making money! They go to work to get paid."

James nodded, saying, "Exactly! Most people do it for the money. They go through life chasing it but are never deeply committed to anything but themselves. For those with the *EntreSpirit*, there's a bigger reason. Let me explain. The statement for principle number one goes like this: **The *EntreSpirit* serves a MISSION, working for a purpose far greater than financial gain, power, or success. Its motivation comes from a strong conviction that they were born to make a difference in the world.**"

The man spoke passionately as he rattled off the statement from memory. Capturing Luke's full attention, he continued. "You see, your mission is why you do your work. It's your cause, and it's deeply personal to you. For example, Henry Ford believed that the automobile should be affordable and within reach of all Americans. That was his mission. It was his big why. He believed it would make transportation easier."

Nodding his head, Luke responded, "I know that story, but his timing was impeccable, and he filled a void that the public didn't know was there. Not everyone can time the market like that or have an ingenious idea to serve the masses. What about the guy that owns a tire shop? Or the lady with a hair salon? Those ideas aren't exactly revolutionary or life-changing. What's their mission supposed to be?"

With confidence, James responded, "You're right. There's nothing world-changing about chocolate either, but Milton Hershey used it to improve the lives of over ten thousand children. I don't know if you're familiar with his story, but he and his wife couldn't have children, so they created a school for orphans. It still exists in Pennsylvania today as the Milton Hershey School. He was so passionate about his school that he left his assets to the school's trust. More mind-boggling is that this trust exists today and has the controlling interest in Hershey, a multibillion-dollar company. You see, business leaders with the *EntreSpirit* can use their profits to fund their mission. Does that make more sense now?"

Luke sighed, saying, "It makes sense, but it doesn't help me any. I didn't have a mission. I didn't give away anything either. I sold my boats to a bunch of rich snobs and stuck-up movie stars. I'm sure we could have helped some people, but that's just not how it worked out for us." Unsure of what else to say, Luke took another deep breath and looked down at the floor.

"Well," James said softly. "It's not too late. Just because you didn't have a mission in the past doesn't mean you can't have one in the future. Besides, it takes time to figure out your mission—sometimes decades. Your mission has to be deeply personal, and it often comes from your experiences in life."

The man's kindly spoken words were meant to be encouraging, but instead, they cut deep into Luke's heart. Not only had he been absent of any missional purpose with CataSail, but more discouraging was the mention of the future. How could he even think about having a mission or purpose with his failures so fresh? Like salt poured on a wound, the task was too painful for him. Unable to respond, Luke continued looking at the floor. His shortcomings and insecurities now visible, he felt like he already failed the first test.

Seeing Luke's demeanor, James decided a change of scenery might be helpful. Standing up, he said, "Gentlemen, let's move along. I'd like to show Luke around, if that's okay?"

Agreeing, Miguel and Luke followed James outside. The village seemed so quiet, almost as if the people had all packed up and moved away. Except for some elderly natives sitting outside the central meeting space, not a soul could be seen. Walking on the boardwalks that connected the buildings, James showed off the village's small library, medical center, and modest grocery store. Coming to the school, James spoke softly, pointing to the classroom full of children sitting inside. As they passed, Miguel stepped on a board that creaked loudly, causing a few kids to giggle. The tour ended with a visit to the central meeting space, which the men quietly entered. Inside were roughly one hundred empty folding chairs and a small stage.

"Do you know what we use this space for, Luke?" James said as they viewed the empty facility.

"Looks like a meeting space to me," Luke responded.

James smiled, deeply admiring it, and said, "Yes, it is. It's also where we hold worship services each weekend. Actually, that's what brought me here."

It took a few seconds to sink in, but when it did, Luke felt like an idiot for not seeing it sooner. Without thinking, he blurted out, "So, you're like some sort of missionary or something?"

James didn't look at Luke when he responded. Instead, he continued admiring the room and said, "Something like that, I guess. At least, that's what people back in the States like to call us. In this village, they call me pastor, or 'padre' in Spanish. But I'm just a regular guy. Most of the time, I see myself as Mr. Montgomery, seventh-grade pre-algebra teacher at Haynes Bridge Middle School—famous for teaching math using transparencies and an overhead projector."

"You were a teacher?" Luke asked curiously.

"Yes. For twenty-five years actually," James answered with a small laugh.

"Wow. So how do you go from being a middle school teacher to a missionary in the middle of the Amazon jungle?"

Again, James chuckled. "That's exactly what I'm trying to teach you. I didn't just wake up one day and say, 'Let's sell everything and move to Peru.' And no, God didn't appear to me and tell us to leave our friends, family, and air-conditioned home. We're here because it's our mission to serve these people and help them live in the best way possible. Teaching was my job for years, but being here is my calling. It's my passion and one of my greatest joys. Sometimes people worry about me back in the States. They think I'm suffering down here, but you know what? I'd rather be here than any place on Earth."

Leaving the gathering space, the men retreated to James' hut, where they ate lunch and continued their discussion. For nearly an hour, Luke's host passionately shared story after story about the villagers' triumphs. When Miguel asked about the future, James joyfully spoke of their expansion efforts. Though Luke wanted to pay attention and focus on his host's words, he struggled to keep up. Saturating his thoughts were the questions that revealed his missionless past. Worse yet, experiencing how enthusiastically James spoke about the village and its future drove the point home all the more. The man was a missionary, not an entrepreneur, but that didn't matter. His infectious zeal overflowed as he spoke, making Luke feel terribly uncomfortable.

As their time came to a close, James decided to share one last thought with Luke. Shaking hands, he said, "Young man, I'll be praying for you. I know you've been through a lot over the last couple of years, and it's easy to get fixated on all the negative things. You'll be tempted to try to get back everything you've lost and focus on yourself. Let me encourage you that the way to happiness isn't backward but forward. Try to let everything go. Find something new. Find your mission and you'll find true happiness."

Luke weakly smiled, thanking his host, and after everyone said goodbye, he followed Miguel down the long wooden dock until they reached the water. Now, oblivious to the jungle, the trees, or the village, Luke could think of nothing but his host's final words as he boarded the narrow canoe-like boat. Ignoring the driver and the powerful engine attached, he sat down on a seat in the center as he questioned his motives. He thought of his host's simple life, living carefree in the middle of a jungle.

Is there anything I care about? Luke thought as the motor started. As they sped along the river, he desperately tried to find something that he or CataSail had done for others, but there was nothing.

Had the weather cooperated, Luke might have thought about the situation for hours. Tapping Luke's leg, Miguel pointed to the ominous thunderstorm clouds forming above. Still speeding forward, giant drops of rain began pelting them as they continued what would be a very long trip back to the plane. Raising his hand to cover his eyes from the painful wet bullets, Luke now understood why they'd have to return by boat.

For six and a half hours, they barely slowed. On and off, the icy rain fell, punishing the boaters as their wet bodies shivered in the wind. By the time they returned to the city, the weary men welcomed dry ground, but their trip wasn't over. A twenty-minute taxi ride would follow, taking the men from the riverbank to the airport. Finally, Luke and Miguel boarded the plane—cold, tired, and wet from their long journey.

7 WELCOME TO THE BIG APPLE

At 7:26 on Tuesday morning, Luke's day started. For the second day in a row, the plane's landing had awoken him. Sitting up and looking out the window next to his bed, he could see the sun breaking through the trees. As they taxied forward, he read a blue sign in the distance, informing him of his location. They'd landed at Teterboro, a small private airport just outside of Manhattan. He'd heard of the airport before but still couldn't believe it. Just yesterday, he was in the middle of the Amazon talking to a missionary. Now he found himself thousands of miles away in an entirely different kind of jungle—the concrete jungle of New York City. Shaking his head, he collapsed back onto his pillow as he thought about his situation.

The plane rolled to a stop about fifty yards from an open hanger. Within a couple of minutes, the sound of men talking along with a loud bang came from the baggage area just behind Luke's cabin. Curious about the commotion, Luke sat up to see a golf cart parked outside. A man dressed in coveralls picked up two flat trays and brought them to the front of the plane. With all the noise, Luke couldn't sleep anyway and decided he'd see if Miguel would tell him about the day's plans. After washing up and brushing his teeth, Luke opened his cabin door. To his surprise, AJ greeted him, now sitting at the table with Miguel.

"You're up early, young man. I'm sorry if we woke you!" AJ's bright tone made it sound like he'd been up for hours.

"Oh! Good morning, sir. I didn't know you were here," Luke responded.

AJ smiled and said, "Actually, I got in late last night. I'm sorry I didn't get to connect with you yesterday, but I hope you had a good day. If you're up to it, grab a seat and have a cup of coffee with us."

Miguel turned Luke's cup over and poured him some coffee from the carafe sitting on the table.

"Thank you, Miguel," Luke said politely as he sat down. "Yesterday was quite an adventure and something I'll never forget, that's for sure."

"Mr. Luke, you had a good time on helicopter, but you didn't like rain though," Miguel said with a smile, reminding Luke of the downpour.

"No. I guess that part wasn't too fun, but the jungle is just mind-bending. I haven't seen anything like it in all my life," Luke said.

"Fantastic, my boy! I'm glad you had a good time. And how is James? Did you enjoy your time with him?"

Luke paused for a second to consider the question. "It was a unique experience, to say the least. James is quite an interesting guy, and we had a good conversation. He seems like he's pretty happy down there."

"He sure is. Now tell me what you learned yesterday about the *EntreSpirit* and having a mission. I want to hear all about it!" AJ continued, sounding very interested in what Luke might have discovered.

"I don't know...I struggled a bit there," Luke said, trying to think through his words. "I frustrated him a bit because...well, it seems I don't really have a mission. I tried thinking more about that last night. Cata-Sail made luxury catamaran sailboats. We were innovative, but a high-tech yacht isn't something people really need. It certainly didn't change the world. I guess if I had taken the company public, or had a billion dollars, I might have been able to do some good, but that just isn't my story, and—"

"No, that's CataSail's story, and that's in your past," AJ said, interrupting Luke. "Forget about that, and let's talk about today. Any thoughts on what your mission might be? I hear you're pretty passionate about drinking beer."

Luke hesitated, now realizing AJ was privy to yesterday's conversation. Feeling unsure of himself and trying to be careful with his words, he finally said, "I guess you heard about our conversation then. I'm trying, AJ, but I don't know what my mission is. I can see why having one might be helpful...but it isn't something I've considered before. To be honest, I don't know if I even understand it from a business point of view. I guess what I'm trying to say is that I don't see how it matters in business. There are plenty of entrepreneurs more successful than I will ever be without a mission."

AJ smiled across the table at Luke and said confidently, "You're exactly right. Most people don't have a mission. That's the problem. They wander through life only serving themselves. They do everything for money, power, or their own vanity, but when things get tough, they'll buckle under the pressure and sabotage the whole thing. To endure, one needs a mission. It's the first part of the *EntreSpirit*—and what we look for in our leaders."

Uneasy with what AJ said, Luke shifted in his seat and with slight sarcasm said, "Well, unfortunately, I don't have a mission. Maybe I'll do better with the other hosts."

AJ let out a chuckle as he shook his head, amused by Luke's response. "You'll get there, my boy. You just don't have a mission yet. The keyword is yet. I think there are a few more things you need to understand about the *EntreSpirit*. For starters, it isn't about business. It's about what makes organizations great. James doesn't own a business, yet he's a fantastic entrepreneur. His mission drives them forward and they're wildly successful at what they do. The problem is that you still think entrepreneurship is only about business, but it's not all dollars and cents. You'll get there, my boy! You'll get there!"

Feeling a bit like he was being lectured by the chipper old man, Luke pointed out the obvious issue that had been bothering him since he met

James yesterday. Unfortunately, he spoke a little more passionately than he intended to. "I don't get it! How can you call James an entrepreneur? He's a former teacher who runs a half-empty village in the jungle. I don't see how that could qualify him. The village was nice and all, and I understand his aim, but he's a missionary—and isn't a mission what he's supposed to have? I'm not trying to be difficult—it just doesn't make sense to call him an entrepreneur."

Luke's bold judgment didn't move AJ, who continued to smile, saying, "Oh my! You've got a long way to go to understand the *EntreSpirit*! Obviously, you don't quite comprehend what James' organization is doing down there or the full extent of his story."

After taking a sip of coffee, AJ became more serious and decided to set the record straight. "So, let me tell you where you're missing it, son, and why James is not only an entrepreneur but also someone you can learn a lot from. You see, James has a brilliant mind. He's not just a math whiz, but he's also a spiritual man, which is how he came up with his mission. That is, to go down to Peru and help the people there. Did he tell you all of that?"

Luke nodded. "He's a missionary, so I figured that was his mission. That's what I was supposed to learn from him, right?"

"Right! But what you're missing is the full extent of their work. He isn't just a single missionary living in the jungle. He's created a movement and leads a very successful organization. A few years ago, he and his family started a nonprofit called Hope for Napo. Each year, they generate millions of dollars in donations, and that money is going back to help jungle villages all across the area. Back in Atlanta, they've got a small office with a few staff members raising money for their cause. They've completely rebuilt the village he lives in now, but next year they'll rebuild two more villages. Within the next two years, he thinks they'll be able to help another five villages rebuild. Within five years, his goal is to rebuild twenty-five more villages. They're also recruiting doctors, nurses, and teachers to come and serve the needs of the area."

Luke slowly slouched in his seat, indicating AJ was divulging new information.

AJ continued, "He's a humble man and won't take credit for how big their organization is growing, but make no mistake about it, he's a strong leader and very entrepreneurial. I'm guessing you also have no idea how he became a missionary then?"

"He told me he was a teacher, but that's about as far as we got," Luke said in his defense. "Most of the time, we talked about my lack of mission."

AJ nodded and said, "Well, let me tell you the story. The seed for everything was planted when he and his wife adopted a little boy from Peru. His name is Josiah, and he was two or three years old when they got him. It was their boy who caused them to learn Spanish and made them interested in the area. A couple of years after the adoption, James organized a mission trip for their local church. They headed down to Peru for two weeks, even bringing some doctors and nurses too. After their first trip, they were hooked. From that point on, they started taking mission trips every summer to help the people. You have to understand that the natives were more primitive back when he first started going. They didn't have medical resources, access to education, or a nice village as you saw yesterday. I'm talking about people who lived deep in the heart of the jungle. It's still extremely remote today but imagine what it was like back then."

AJ paused as he thought about the story. Slowly lifting his coffee, he took another sip.

"So that's how he became a missionary then?"

AJ nodded and said, "That's how they started visiting, but that's not how they found the village you were at yesterday. Did he tell you about that trip?"

Luke shook his head, unaware of the story.

"Well, one spring, they heard about this tribe who'd lost everything. Apparently, the river went to a record flood level and wiped out every building they had. The plan was to find the village and help them rebuild. They had also brought medical supplies and financial resources. But that's not how things worked out. Because the people had moved further inland, the team had a hard time finding them. As they searched, James ended up getting whacked in the face with a machete. I don't know all the details, but the cut was pretty bad. I think he needed like twenty stitches or something. It might have been a big deal, but they had a doctor on the team. He stitched him up and they continued."

"So that's how he got the scar on his face?" Luke asked, pointing to his cheek.

"Yes, but after the stitches, he was fine. However, that scar was a turning point for him. You see, when he and his team got to the village, they were shocked at its condition. The people were starving, drinking dirty water, and wearing the same clothes for days on end. Because almost everything they owned had been destroyed in the flood, they tried to rebuild further inland. I don't know what you know about jungle living, but the river is the people's source of food and life, so being further inland wasn't good for the tribe. To hear James tell it, he says it was the worst thing he'd ever seen, and there were easily fifteen people sleeping in each little hut. It was a mess—I'm talking about deplorable living conditions."

As Luke listened, he considered how courageous James and his team must have been. He pictured their mosquito-bitten bodies bushwhacking through the jungle. Drenched by the rain and trudging through the mud, they searched for the village. *How much money had they spent in the search?* Luke shook his head at how selfish he'd been at times. Immersed in the story, his coffee cup remained full.

AJ's eyes glazed over as he stared off into the distance. "So, that's how they found the village you were at yesterday. Do you want to know what caused them to go and live down there permanently?"

"Please!" Luke responded, now fully invested in learning more about the missionary.

AJ smiled. "Well, his team might have been feeling bad for the villagers, but when the people saw the cut on James' face, his stitches, and his bloody clothes, they felt just as bad for him. And despite how poor they were and the little they had, they poured out gift after gift to thank his team for coming. Here he sat, feeling sorry for the tribe, but they felt sorry for him and were willing to give him the shirts off of their backs. It had a profound impact on him and his family. Within six months, he and his wife sold everything and quit their jobs. They just showed up one day with their bags, ready to move in and work. They've been down there about four years. Since then, their family has helped those people immensely. They've rebuilt the entire village above the flood line. They've added a hospital, library, and school. Five days a week, all the able men and women head out in teams. Two groups go into the jungle to collect plants and specimens for medical research while another group goes fishing."

"So that's why the village was so empty yesterday?" Luke thought out loud.

AJ set down his coffee cup as he mentally calculated the hours Luke would have been there. "That's right. They all return home a little after three o'clock, so it would have been pretty empty when you were there. Anyway, James was your first host because he exemplifies the *EntreSpirit* and the importance of having a mission. I hope that makes a little more sense to you now."

Out of respect for AJ and the missionary, Luke now spoke more carefully. He knew that AJ admired the man's work, and offered, "I guess I shouldn't have judged him without knowing all he's done down there. I just didn't consider…I mean, before hearing his story, I wouldn't have considered James an entrepreneur."

AJ drove the point home. "Exactly! But he's as much of an entrepreneurial leader as anyone starting a business from scratch. Heck, he had to travel two thousand miles just to open up shop! His mission is just different. It isn't money that drives him, but a community of hurting people in the jungle. Out of thin air, his family created a dramatic change in a broken-down village. No more lice or poverty. No one dying because they don't have access to antibiotics or clean water. The irony of it all is that he feels fortunate to be there and tells people that the village changed his life. It helped him find his calling. The *EntreSpirit* isn't what it seems, but when you fully understand it, you'll discover some of the best entrepreneurs in the world aren't just business owners doing it for the money. They're people in all walks of life doing what they do because it's their mission."

"So, you believe entrepreneurs exist in nonprofits then too? People like Mother Teresa?" Luke added.

"Absolutely!" AJ responded as he looked at his watch. "**The *EntreSpirit* serves a MISSION, working for a purpose far greater than financial gain, power, or success. Its motivation comes from a strong conviction that they were born to make a difference in the world.** But you've got four more pieces of the puzzle to put together, son. There are more hosts you need to meet. You'd best be getting dressed for the day. We've gotta get you fed, through customs, and into the Bronx by noon."

Miguel, who had sat silently listening, now headed to the galley. He then returned with a coat hanger covered by a frosted plastic bag. "Mr. Luke, I have clothes for you. Today is a beautiful sunny day in city. You go to a baseball game and meet your next friend and host. Mr. Aaron is a very funny man. You like sports, Mr. Luke, so you have a good time with Mr. Aaron. I think you will like him very much."

By a quarter till ten, Luke had showered, dressed, and finished his breakfast. After a quick chat with a customs agent onboard, he departed the plane. The unusually warm spring temperature, sunshine, and budding trees made the day that much better. His transportation, a pristine black stretch limousine, sat waiting outside of the private terminal. After greeting Luke, the driver opened the door, allowing him to be seated. Today, he'd travel to meet his host alone, but he didn't care. Dressed in blue jeans, a pinstripe jersey, and a dark navy cap, he already knew where he was going. Like a kid in a candy store, he couldn't stop smiling. The ticket in his hand told him everything he needed to know. *New York Yankees versus Toronto Blue Jays.* Somehow, he'd be meeting his host in a private suite to watch baseball at iconic Yankee Stadium. Though Luke didn't consider himself a Yankees fan and had never been to the stadium, he loved the game of baseball.

"Guess where I am?" Luke said, holding his phone to his ear. After a brief moment, he yelled, "NEW YORK CITY! I'm in a limo headed to Yankee Stadium. Can you believe it, babe? They got me on suite level too! Oh honey, wait until I tell you about my trip. I've been to Dallas, the Amazon jungle, and now I am in New York City. They're flying me in a private jet with my own suite and shower." Luke's excitement became uncorked. Realizing he hadn't been very thoughtful, he added, "I miss you, babe. How are you? How are the boys?"

For the next thirty minutes, Luke caught up with his wife, filling her in on his journey. Without taking a breath, he poured out every detail of his private jet ride and executive cabin. He laughed as he spoke of Miguel and AJ, and their interesting but unusual conversations. With all of Luke's excitement, it took his wife nearly five minutes to put the trip in chronological order. She didn't mind though. She heard something in her husband's voice that'd gone missing. He seemed excited again. It was more than just baseball—he was excited to be doing something, to be going somewhere. It was as if something that had been asleep in him was starting to wake up, and for the briefest of moments, she felt like she had her old Luke back. As he crossed the Alexander Hamilton Bridge and went south on I-87, he could see the stadium in the distance. Giddy, like a little boy, he promised to call her back as soon as he could and hung up the phone to take in the views.

8 OVERCOMING IN THE BRONX

Luke hopped out a few steps past 161st Street and headed towards the glass double doors with a large silver sign that read *Suite Entrance*. Still an hour before game time, Yankee Stadium was buzzing outside. Whizzing through security and up the escalator, he could hardly wait to explore. To his surprise, the suite-level walkway that surrounded the stadium was fairly quiet—except for a few professionally dressed ushers who greeted him. Life-sized black and white photos of Yankee legends adorned the navy blue and gray walls. To identify each suite, bright silver numbers hung outside the frosted glass doors. Reaching number twenty-five, Luke noticed the small card on the wall identifying the suite owner, *Hickson Prosthetics*.

"Wow! They did this right!" Luke said out loud as he inspected the empty room. Travertine tile covered the foyer floor and granite counters adorned the kitchen area, which was already well-stocked with an array of delights. High pile plush carpet, Italian leather chairs, and a large glass coffee table followed, creating a living room atmosphere. Legendary Yankee history, forever captured in photos, lined the walls to the end of the suite. Overlooking the playing field, a glass wall connected to a granite counter allowed those desiring air conditioning to watch the game from inside. As Luke opened the door to explore the outdoors, he discovered two rows of five cushioned seats. On the field below, players stretched while the grounds crew worked to make the field ready.

Returning inside, Luke smiled as he continued to inspect the pictures on the wall. Though he wanted to drink a beer and watch the players, he thought it more polite to wait patiently for his host. Sitting down on one of the leather chairs, he pulled out his phone to check his messages. Like most days, the collection calls were constant, and he could see that he had nine new voicemails. Without listening to the messages, Luke began deleting each one until he came to a voicemail from his old CFO. Luke started to read the transcribed message, but because he sat alone in the suite, he decided to play it out loud.

"Luke, it's Johnathan. I hope you're doing well. Listen, I know we haven't talked in a while, but I had something weird happen today and I wanted to give you a heads up. Two suits came to my job asking to see me. The receptionist let them in because they showed badges like they were cops. Then they started asking a bunch of questions about you and CataSail. I smelled BS right away, and when I asked to see their badges, they explained that they were private detectives. I kicked their asses out in a hurry, but I wanted you to know that something's up. Give me a shout when you get this. I hope everything is okay. Give my best to your family. Thanks."

Whatever optimism Luke had mustered evaporated in an instant. He sat back in his chair as he exhaled a deep breath. Now he knew for a fact that JROB Holdings was digging for dirt and would likely try to incriminate him. Luke's thoughts turned dark quickly as he reflected on his investors. His valiant effort to save the company wasn't enough. They wanted to break him and leave him with nothing but the skin on his back. Upset with himself for checking the message in the first place, he shoved his phone back into his pants and continued to stew, and within a few minutes, he was boiling mad. It was the worst possible time too—at 12:17, the door to Suite 25 opened up, revealing Luke's second host.

Standing up, Luke met eyes with a black athletic man—standing a couple of inches over six feet. Appearing to be in his mid-fifties, he smiled at Luke as the door closed behind him. Dressed in a gray baseball jersey, Luke noticed his smooth bald head and muscular pectoral muscles that protruded from his shirt. The man continued towards Luke until he cleared the granite counters, now revealing his lower body. The man's jean shorts allowed Luke to notice his left leg was absent. In its place, a black and silver prosthetic leg supported him.

"I'm guessing you're Luke?" the man said as he approached.

"Yes, sir, I am. Nice to meet you," Luke responded, intentionally trying not to stare at his lower torso.

"I'm Aaron Hickson," the man said, shaking Luke's hand. "Always good to meet another entrepreneur. I hope I haven't kept you waiting too long."

"No, sir. I just got here a few minutes ago. I've been exploring your suite a bit."

"Perfect. We've got about forty minutes until game time. That should be all we need. Do you want to grab a drink or a snack before we get started?"

"Sounds good. I'll have whatever you're having," Luke responded, hoping it would be an ice-cold beer.

"Water for me. I'm trying to stay in shape, but it's getting harder and harder as I get older. Have whatever you want, Luke. Seriously, it's all included."

The two men perused the stocked kitchen, each filling up a small plate of food and adding a water bottle. Returning to their seats, Aaron opened up the conversation. "I'm guessing you know why you're here and that it's my job to see if you've got the *EntreSpirit*. Who have you met so far?"

"I met AJ, Miguel, and the pilots on Sunday. Yesterday, I was with James down in Peru. That's it so far," Luke answered without hesitation.

"Okay, so, you're just getting started—that's good! You haven't met everybody yet, so let me tell you how this works. Those guys are the nice guys. They say I'm the mean one because I'm here to push your buttons. I'm going to ask you some tough questions. Fair warning—I'm going to be very direct. I want you to know that I'm not trying to be offensive, but I'm going to dig for the truth. I'd encourage you to be honest with me and say what's on your mind. You can say whatever you want to me and I promise I won't be offended. Sound good?"

"Okaaaay," Luke said uneasily as he put down his plate to focus.

"First of all, tell me why you're so out of shape? I noticed that right away. Are you undisciplined, or simply afraid of hard work?" Aaron's tone strengthened as he fired his first question.

"Well, I used to work out four times a week. But—" Luke started to respond before he was interrupted.

"But then what? You quit and got fat? I'd think a successful entrepreneur like yourself would be tougher than that! Was the company paying for your gym membership or something?" Aaron said with a condescending tone.

Almost as if he suffered from a personality disorder, Luke's host had transformed from a normal nice guy to a schoolyard bully in seconds. Trying to stay cool and fight off his anger, Luke smoothly responded, "It's been a tough season, as you have probably seen on the news. And no, I didn't lose the membership. It's just—"

Interrupting again, Aaron pounced to finish his sentence. "It's just you're not committed. That is, to taking care of yourself and your family. You're just letting it all go, I hear. Is that right?"

Luke didn't flinch outwardly, but the jab about not taking care of his family stung deeply. "Maybe for a season, Aaron. I guess I like to eat a little too much. As I said, it's been a tough year for us," he said, trying to soften the mood.

Aaron didn't take the bait. Instead, he changed the subject and now picked at the healing scab called CataSail. "Tell me why you closed shop. What's it been, almost a year now? Was it just too much pressure?"

"Well, obviously it wasn't something I wanted to do. But when you run out of money—"

"You fight like hell to raise more!" Aaron shouted at Luke. For the third time, he rudely interrupted his guest. "Come on! There had to be something you could have done!"

This time, Luke's tone grew louder and bolder, but he continued to remain calm. "I did everything I could to stay open. The problem, in case you didn't see it all over the news, was a little bigger than we expected."

"Yeah, we all saw you on TV. You were pretty famous for a while there. So, is that it then? Is that the end of you? Are you done fighting? You going to lay down and die, let your wife marry some other dude and raise your kids?" It was now clear that Aaron's job was to rattle contestants and try to break them.

Luke could feel his face growing flush as the man jabbed below the belt again. Deciding he'd had enough and would apply pressure to his host, Luke responded confidently, now going on the attack. "What kind of dumbass questions are these? I guess Stanton can't figure out his own business. He needs some help, so he sends a muscle head that doesn't know anything about business. I know you think you know me, but you don't. And obviously, neither of you know much about business or what I've been through."

Aaron didn't flinch. Instead, he took Luke's words as a challenge. "So, you think you know how this works? I'm asking tough questions because we need to know if you got what it takes. You want me to be soft? You want me to coddle you like a baby? To give you a little bottle and change your poopy diaper? You don't need that. Trust me, you need someone to tell you the truth. Maybe this contest isn't for you."

The man's continued disrespect burned deep inside Luke, and he retaliated in the most sarcastic tone he could muster. "Well, maybe you're right. I'm just here for the free beer and food. What makes you think I want to be part of your little club anyway? And you're right. I've put on a few pounds. I'm not perfect. You want to know what else? Our company killed a senator. Yep, we blew his ass up! Oh, wait—no, we didn't. It was an ACCIDENT! But that doesn't matter because the whole world doesn't care about that part. You didn't mention my friend, Dellin—our

COO who died in the explosion. Nobody cared about his death, did they? Do you want to ask me about him too?"

"You done, bro?" Aaron said, ignoring Luke's sarcasm.

Luke wasn't done. "Let's see what else I can share—oh yeah, my marriage is struggling too. Yep, we've been fighting. Why? Because I can't pull my shit together. Doctors say I might have a touch of depression. What else? How about my kids? Yes, they miss me because I'm too wrapped up in trying to figure it out. And if all that ain't enough, I'm getting sued by my investors and LOSING EVERYTHING! So, yeah, it's pretty shitty—'bro.'"

Aaron wouldn't let Luke surrender. In a slightly softer tone, he started in again. "I'm sorry about your friend. You can feel bad about him, but that's it. You think you got it hard? You don't know what hard is. Sitting up in your fancy house and fancy boat. Driving your fancy cars worried about getting sued. You want me to feel sorry for you? Is that it? Man up and STOP BEING A BOY! So the world took a dump on you. Are you going to stay in the toilet and get flushed down with the rest of the shit? Or are you gonna climb out and fight? That's what we all want to know."

That was it—Luke had taken enough and contemplated punching the man in the face. He might have done so, had he thought he'd win the fight. Instead, he decided to give the man one more piece of his mind. In the softest of voices, he said, "I might not have this stupid *EntreSpirit* thing, or whatever you want to call it. I might even be the biggest loser in the world." Then, in contrast, Luke raised his voice to a yell. Looking Aaron directly in the eyes, he spewed his honest thoughts. "I might be all of those things, but YOU are a FREAKING JERK! Contest or no contest, YOU'RE the biggest asshole I have EVER MET! My situation will change, and I will get back on my feet again. I will build another business and be successful again—but you'll STILL be JUST AN ASSHOLE!"

It wasn't worthy of an Academy Award, but Luke's emphatic speech sure made him feel better. Most men would have shied away or said the words under their breath as they walked out, but not Luke. He sat there confidently, fists balled up and ready to brawl if needed. Resolving it would take multiple security officers to remove him, he smirked at his rival as if to say, "What are you going to do now?"

To Luke's surprise, his host was grinning. Slowly, he put his hands together, making the sound of a single clap. Then he added another, and then another. Soon the man was clapping loudly. Standing up, he smiled and reached out to shake Luke's hand. "Now that's what I'm talking about, man!"

Luke held out his hand in response, still confused by the situation. Now sitting back down, Aaron's tone changed as he returned to the perfect gentleman Luke had met upon arrival.

"I apologize for being so confrontational. The way I asked you those questions was very aggressive, and I won't interrupt you anymore. You don't understand this just yet, but it was important for us to put pressure on you. It might sound crazy, but it's my job to see if you can overcome it. That's part of the *EntreSpirit*."

Confused, Luke scratched his head and said, "All of that was the *EntreSpirit*? Being rude and telling me off?"

"Not telling you off, but gauging your ability to overcome based upon your response. We're looking for people who will get up when they fall and continue to fight. That's the second part of the *EntreSpirit*. It might sound crazy, but that whole thing was to see what you're made of and how you react under pressure," Aaron said as he took a sip of his water, now calm and relaxed.

"So, you were just trying to ruffle my feathers? You didn't mean any of those words?" Luke asked, trying to cool off.

"No, I meant those words. Every one of them! I am curious why you're out of shape and why your company folded. Also, I'm truly sorry about your friend—but at the same time, I believe that people shouldn't be babied when they go through hard times. Business is hard. So is life. So, I meant everything I said, but the way I spoke was pretty rude." Aaron's response was honest, but his tone now had empathy.

Aaron continued, now hoping to bring clarity. "Let me explain. My role in the contest is to see if you have the *EntreSpirit* and the ability to overcome. The statement goes like this: **The *EntreSpirit* OVERCOMES. It considers setbacks and failures as part of the journey. Its relentless work ethic and commitment to win allow it to move forward despite adversity.** Luke, you've faced a painful situation, and it's perfectly normal to need a season to recover. At the same time, we have to know if you'll—"

"What? Get up again? Fight back? Recover from this disaster?" Luke interrupted sarcastically.

"Will you?" Aaron asked humbly.

Leaning forward, Luke ran his fingers through his hair. It might have been because of Aaron's tough questions or because of the news that his investors were digging for dirt, but either way, Luke didn't have an answer. Instead, the broken man spoke emotionally about his past. "I couldn't figure it out. I should have done things differently. Dellin shouldn't have been on the boat. When we got in trouble, I could have stopped the expansion. I should have thought through things more carefully—if I had, things might be different. It all just happened so damn fast."

No longer applying pressure to his guest, Aaron spoke softly. "Come on Luke…those were tough decisions. Decisions that most CEOs wouldn't be able to make with certainty. Let me ask you something. Did you do everything you could—believing the impossible, fighting, sacrificing, clawing, scratching, biting, and scrambling, to keep the company afloat? I'm talking about 110 percent?"

"Yes, even cashing in my retirement accounts and personally signing for the debt to keep us alive. After Dellin died, I practically lived there. I fought hard and—"

Aaron promised not to interrupt, but he couldn't help it and said loudly, "Then let it go, man! If you did everything you could do, LET IT GO! Bury it—and move on! You owe it to yourself, and your family." Though his tone was strong, Luke, who now looked down at the floor, could hear the sincerity in his host's voice.

Without hesitating, Aaron continued. "I know this is some tough stuff, but I want to tell you something that might encourage you. I don't tell too many people this, but I think it will help because you got some deep wounds. You see this leg here? I lost it when I was ten years old in an automobile accident. A drunk driver ran a red light and t-boned us. My dad died instantly, and I lost my left leg."

"I'm so sorry to hear that," Luke said softly as he looked up and processed his host's adversities.

"My dad was my best friend. He loved baseball and the New York Yankees. We used to go to games together. Before that day, I had only one dream in my childish mind—it was to pitch in the major leagues for this baseball team. I was good too. Probably would've made it had I not gotten in the accident. I could throw a sixty-five-mile-per-hour fastball at ten years old. I was so fast that our high school coach was talking to my dad about me playing. He said that with my speed, I might make it to the pros one day. When my dad died, and I lost my leg, I quit baseball. I quit everything. I sat in my room and cried for months."

"I...I'm sorry, man. I can't imagine how hard that must have been," Luke said respectfully.

Aaron continued as he looked down at his missing leg. "I would have kept on like that, but my mom said something that got me thinking. She said that my dad was up in heaven watching me, and whatever I did in life, he'd be proud of me. So, I started thinking about what I could do. In baseball, lefties push off from their left leg when they pitch. So, with my prosthetic, I still couldn't pitch. One day, I was sitting out in PE watching the other kids play, and I had the idea to change pitching arms and start throwing with my right hand. It was like I heard the idea deep down inside and I felt so excited to go home and try it out. You want to know what happened?"

Now enraptured with the story, Luke responded, "Of course! So, you just changed pitching arms?"

"Yes, and I sucked. I must have fallen twenty times that first day. It took me three months for it to feel normal, but I kept going. I'd come home every day and throw a hundred pitches. Sometimes I'd throw two hundred. Day after day, I never missed. Mom saw how good I was getting, and the whole family chipped in for me to get a new prosthetic leg, custom made for pitching." Aaron paused as he remembered the story. A huge smile covered his face as his mind traveled back in time.

Continuing the tale, Aaron spoke even softer. "I'm not the biggest guy in the world, but one thing I am is driven. When I set my mind to something, I never give up. It took longer than I wanted, but in about a year, I was almost as fast as before the accident. Because I had to relearn everything from scratch, I was more aware of my body, and my control was much better with my right hand. By the time I was 13, I could strike out a lot of high schoolers. When I was in high school, I struck out everybody. I ended up getting a full scholarship to play ball for Princeton. Though I didn't make it to the pros, I did get a great education. The truth is, I would never be where I'm at today if I had given up."

Luke, now full of respect, offered, "I guess that's how you got into prosthetics too?"

Aaron looked up and laughed. "Ha! That's another story, my man, but it's a good one. Out of college, I started selling prosthetics. It seemed like a great idea because of having a prosthetic myself—sort of like I was an expert in the business. I did well, and two years later, I went out on my own, investing everything I had in inventory. It went pretty well for a couple of years, but then we started to expand. In turn, when I kept slow paying my line of credit, the bank cut me off. The rest of the story is ugly. We ended up folding, and I lost everything. I had to start all over, so that's how I got started in prosthetics."

Luke chuckled. "So you've got some battle wounds too? I'm glad I'm not the only one!"

"Yes, I do, and that's why I won't let people whine about how difficult it is! You'll probably understand this, but some people see my success and money and they think it all came easy for me. They don't see the tough times I've faced, and how hard I've worked to get where I am. There ain't anything easy about business! Well, I'm proud to say that we reached three hundred million in revenues last year, and we're the third-largest provider of athletic grade prosthetics in the world."

Luke smiled, thankful to hear of Aaron's achievements. "Nice comeback! Congrats on your success, man. I can see why they've got you talking about overcoming adversity."

Aaron continued, "Thanks! I appreciate that, but adversity doesn't make anyone great. So many people face hard times and still give up. They become bitter, shrivel up, and die thinking their world hasn't been fair. They become victims of their circumstances—not overcomers. It isn't adversity that makes someone great, but the mindset that they will overcome. Your story isn't over. The adversity you've faced can make you stronger if you let it. I'm tough on people because I want to encourage them to keep fighting. Now, it's almost game time—you ready for some baseball?"

For the next three hours, the men would enjoy the game together. The smell of fresh-cut grass and the sound of a wooden bat cracking a ball helped Luke forget his troubles. Like two old friends, they ate chicken wings and sipped cold beers together, ignoring their previous conflict and harsh words. Being vulnerable to reveal their battle wounds and scars wasn't easy, but it connected the two kindred spirits with mutual respect for one another. They knew entrepreneurship and all that comes with it. From the glory of victory to the bitter taste of defeat, it had united the men and formed a bond.

As the game neared its end, Luke looked over at his host. Little did Aaron know how his story had profoundly affected Luke. Almost like a fellow soldier, Aaron seemed to arrive on a special mission. There on the battlefield of entrepreneurship, Luke was wounded and left for dead. Though his condition critical, the enemy continued the onslaught of discouragement, threats, and lawsuits. Just when he thought defeat was imminent, Aaron showed up. He was tough as nails—a drill sergeant comfortable in battle and familiar with pain. He didn't flinch at a comrade's grotesque wounds. Instead, he smacked Luke in the face and ordered him to get up. When Luke continued to wallow in his misery, Aaron threw him over his shoulder and carried him back to safety.

It was something that Luke never expected, but there was a spark, allowing his mindset to shift. Starting with just a flicker, a righteous fire began to roar inside of him. For the first time in eighteen months, he felt like fighting back. Though the painful memories of his past would still be present, somehow he would move on. Slowly, he would begin to forgive himself. Whatever JROB Holdings was doing was no longer important. Deep inside, he knew the only thing that mattered was the future version of himself—and that version would be better. That version would somehow—and someway—try to fight back and arise from the ashes.

"Strike three! You're out!" the umpire yelled. And just like that, the game ended.

As Luke exited the stadium and was seated in the limo, he felt determined to overcome, and he knew right where he should start. As the driver pulled away, he opened his phone and dialed a familiar number. Though already saved in his list of contacts, he dialed it from memory: 212-656-3000. The auto-attendant picked up, and without listening to a word, Luke punched in extension 225. Not yet sure of what he'd say, he held his breath and waited for an answer. Luke exhaled in relief as he listened to the mailbox greeting. "You've reached the voicemail of Mike Bird. I'm sorry I can't take your call right now, but please leave a message and I'll return your call as soon as possible. You can also email me at mike.bird@JROBholdings.com—beep."

"Mike. Hey…it's Luke. I know we haven't talked in a while, but I'd like to have a quick chat. I'm traveling this week but will be home on Monday. We received the lawsuit last week and we've also been in touch with your attorneys. I'd like to try to work something out before it gets too ugly. Give me a shout when you get a chance, or I'll try to follow up on Monday of next week. Thanks."

Had the man picked up, Luke had no idea what he would have said. He was thankful to leave a message and that he'd kept his cool. The investment group was suing him, but that didn't matter—he knew he had to face them.

📍 9 BREAKFAST ON THE 17ᵀᴴ

Luke rolled over and picked up the ringing telephone. The automated wake-up message informed him it was 6:30 in the morning. Flipping off his covers, Luke stood up and stretched. Though it was early, he felt well rested and was thankful for a good night's sleep in a comfortable bed. The boutique hotel, located on Manhattan's Upper East Side, had given him a chance to relax and talk with his wife and kids after the game. Today, he'd be meeting his guides for breakfast and then jetting off to meet his third host.

After an average cup of coffee provided by the in-room coffeepot, Luke opened his garment bag for the day. His wardrobe included a pair of blue jeans and a black T-shirt sporting a pink ribbon along with the words: *Support Breast Cancer*. The shirt made him imagine who he would meet, knowing there must be a connection with its message. After a hot shower, he quickly dressed, and by a quarter past seven o'clock, he was ready to head out the door.

Luke gathered his suitcase and unplugged his charging phone. A new text message caught his attention, most likely delivered while he was in the shower. The sender's name immediately caused him to freeze as he unlocked his phone and began to read.

I got your voicemail this morning. To be honest with you, I'm not sure what can be done with your situation. We can talk when you get a chance, but at this point, it's kind of out of my hands and with our attorneys. My suggestion is that you do what they're asking and surrender your assets. Call me if you'd like to discuss this when you get a chance.

Luke sat down on the bed as he finished reading the message. His blood now heating, Luke vented his frustrations out loud, as if the investment group was sitting across from him. "You guys are so full of shit. It's out of your hands? PLEASE! Who do you think I am? You all know I did everything I could do and that still wasn't enough." Exasperated by JROB Holdings' response, Luke fell backward onto his bed. Any part of him who hoped for an amicable resolution with his investors was now gone. Though he vowed to overcome, the demons had returned overnight to torment him. Picturing the investment group's faces, his anger churned inside as he thought about their intentions to incriminate him. For nearly ten minutes, he stewed, contemplating sending a snarky response. He would have sat there longer, but Miguel called, asking him if he was coming to breakfast.

Now ten minutes tardy, Luke stood up. He hated being late but decided it wasn't the end of the world and quickly exited his room. Feeling a little flustered, Luke tried to gather himself and focus on the elegance of the small privately-owned hotel. Though upscale and luxurious, its name was unfamiliar and unassociated with the large hotel brands. The lobby—which seemed more like a living room—was tastefully decorated with cloth chesterfield couches and chairs. Facing the front desk, a large, finely stitched area rug covered the marble floors. As he continued, Luke paused to inspect a giant black and white portrait of a seemingly ordinary girl. Now approaching the front desk, he spotted Miguel quietly waiting for him. Miguel, also on the lookout for Luke, made eye contact and waved him over.

"Good Morning, Miguel. I apologize for being late," Luke said, stretching out his hand to Miguel's.

"Mr. Luke! Good morning, sir. It's okay. Are you ready to eat now? AJ is here and will meet us for breakfast. He is interested in your talk with Mr. Aaron yesterday," Miguel continued to speak as they walked. "And today, we have another special time for you. You meet our friend—Dr. Torres. She is a wonderful researcher of cancer and very warm. You'll like her very much."

With the chime of the elevator, the men entered and zipped up to the seventeenth floor. The absence of guests allowed Luke to respond to Miguel. "A cancer doctor, huh? I guess that explains my shirt. You keep telling me how nice these people are, but I'm not sure you and I are in the same contest," Luke said as he considered his confrontational host from yesterday.

As the doors opened, a well-dressed butler greeted the men. Continuing down the hallway, they reached a finely polished pewter-colored door that Miguel unlocked by swiping his keycard. Upon entering, the immaculate, spacious penthouse suite came into view with its white walls and tasteful decor. Immediately, Luke's eyes were drawn to the glass French doors, which were open wide, providing breathtaking views of the city. Though Luke would have loved a tour of the penthouse suite, Miguel proceeded outside to the terrace. Luke followed, noticing the wooden tiles that covered the outdoor patio floor and freshly painted railing. Dozens of potted plants precisely placed against a brick wall balanced the space, which also offered multiple padded loungers to enjoy the sights of Central Park.

"Good morning, gentlemen," AJ's voice rang out. "How was your baseball game?" Now dressed in another plaid flannel shirt, AJ sat at a linen-covered table with three place settings. It was another beautiful day in New York, and Luke was excited that the men would be eating outside.

"The baseball game? Well, that part was great," Luke responded as he sat down in his chair, knowing that AJ most likely knew about how confrontational Aaron could be.

"I'm glad you enjoyed it. And I'm curious—how is Aaron? Did you guys have a nice discussion?"

"He's good—very direct, but good. He shared with me his story, and we ended up having a pretty good time," Luke answered and then took a sip of coffee, freshly poured by one of the servers.

"He's been through a lot in his life. I'm sure he shared with you the statement for principle number two. **The *EntreSpirit* OVERCOMES. It considers setbacks and failures as part of the journey. Its relentless work ethic and commitment to win allow it to move forward despite adversity.**"

"Yeah, I heard something like that, I guess. You guys seem to have a special statement for everything. I'm just not sure I understand," Luke said, pausing and taking a deep breath. He leaned back in his chair and stared down at his coffee, not intending to continue.

AJ gave him a few seconds before he spoke up. "Don't be discouraged, young man. It is perfectly normal to have setbacks at some point. Every entrepreneur, no matter who they are, will stumble along the way. You're going to make it though. We've all had our share of setbacks. I remember when I—"

Lifting his hand to stop AJ, Luke interrupted. "Thanks, AJ, but you don't need to encourage me. I understand. Entrepreneurs fall and they get back up. They dust themselves off, get back on the horse, and do it again. They're supposed to be tough! They're supposed to fight. They're badass missionaries who thrive in piranha-infested waters. They're one-legged pitchers with huge muscles. I get it! I need to be tougher!"

Swallowing his food before he spoke, AJ looked at Luke and said delicately, "Respectfully, young man, there's more to it than that. I don't think you quite understand what I was going to say, but that's fine if you don't want to hear it." Then he continued to eat his breakfast.

After a short pause, Luke finally spoke up. "I'm sorry, AJ. I shouldn't have said that. I don't mean any disrespect, and I do want to hear what you have to say. It's just...the last couple of years have been difficult, and everyone seems to have an opinion about what I should have done. Sometimes people try to encourage me when they don't understand what I've faced and what I'm going through. I know they mean well. It's just, I don't know..." Luke's words trailed off again. Though guarded, he sincerely wanted to hear what AJ had to say.

AJ smiled at his young contestant, realizing it was a perfect moment to teach him something. "Luke, we aren't here to judge your past—you'll find it's your past that caused us to seek you out. What I'm about to say might sound a little strange, but everyone at Stanton Enterprises encourages failure. We actually won't bring anyone on board who doesn't know what it is like to taste some sort of setback. We think it is good for the soul because setbacks kill arrogance and pride. We like to say, fail early and fail often. And if you ain't failing, you're probably not taking enough risks. I think the problem is that you've been taking your situation personally. You're not seeing failure for what it is. You see the business closing as the end—like it is done and over with."

Luke couldn't help but snicker. "So, you think there's a future for CataSail, huh? We're gonna make a comeback or something?"

AJ shook his head. "No, you're not hearing me right, son. I'm not talking about CataSail, I'm talking about YOU—Luke Voightmann. CataSail is finished, but you, young man, are not! The problem is that you're over-identifying with CataSail and your loss. You're taking the company's failure personally, which is keeping you from seeing the truth right in front of your nose."

Becoming even more sarcastic, Luke responded boldly, "Truth—what truth? Bankruptcy? Lawsuits and judgments? That's the only truth I see."

AJ laughed out loud, which also caused Miguel to join him. Putting down his fork, AJ continued with a big grin across his face. "Well, those are some real problems, son, but it's not the end of the world and certainly not what I'm talking about. You've got to start looking at things differently. Henry Ford said that failure is simply the opportunity to begin again—this time more intelligently. You're acting like your life is over, when the truth is, you're just getting started. Ford's first companies didn't make it, but he didn't give up. Walt Disney's Laugh-O-Gram Studios went bankrupt, but that didn't stop him. Have you heard of Bill Gates' company called Traf-O-Data? Well, that company didn't make it either, but it was foundational in preparing him for Microsoft. How about September 16, 1985, when Steve Jobs got fired from the company he founded? Did you know he said getting fired from Apple was the best thing that could have ever happened to him?"

Though AJ was an older man, his mind was sharp and witty like a teenager, and Luke was instantly sucked into the narration. Like an old country preacher, AJ continued orating, telling story after story of proprietors who failed miserably and then bounced back. "Warren Buffett was rejected from Harvard at age nineteen. That didn't stop him. James Dyson spent five years of his life and made 5,127 prototypes of his vacuum cleaner before he got it right. What if he would have quit? James Patterson was rejected thirty-one times with his first novel. Colonel Sanders, at age sixty-five, started all over. Legend has it that his recipe was rejected over one thousand times before he caught a break and started Kentucky Fried Chicken. Thomas Edison failed over and over again before perfecting the light bulb—and you know what he said? He said, 'many of life's failures are people who did not realize how close they were to success when they gave up.' I've faced failure too, and I've had investors breathing down my neck. And you know what? I'm a better man for it! It didn't kill me, and you're not gonna die either!"

For the next five minutes, AJ continued to rattle off business statistics and stories of first-generation millionaires to encourage Luke. AJ's passion was intoxicating, and everyone, including the two servers, listened to him speak. Finally, his voice softened, and he said, "I could go on and on, son, but do you understand what I'm saying?" AJ picked his fork back up to eat his now cold breakfast.

"I guess you're telling me I'm in good company," Luke confirmed.

AJ leaned forward with a last piece of advice. He spoke more gently and looked Luke right in the eyes. "You've got your whole life ahead of you, and it isn't time to give up. Setbacks and failures are all part of the journey. Every entrepreneur worth their salt will have plenty of failures and ideas that didn't make it. I've had them. You've had them. We've all had them. The *EntreSpirit* doesn't consider failure as final, and it doesn't take those failures personally. It's all par for the course. We know failures will come and we expect them. The *EntreSpirit's* commitment is to overcome. Come hell or high water, and regardless of the odds, that spirit will keep fighting to win! You saw that spirit in James and it's the same spirit you saw in Aaron yesterday. Does that make any sense?"

Luke nodded, still processing as he responded, "I...I understand what you're saying, and you're right, it doesn't make sense to give up. I guess it is hard sometimes because I never dreamed I'd be in this position. You're saying it is good to fail, but if you screw up in the business world, you get fired or go bankrupt. Nobody teaches entrepreneurs to expect setbacks or how to respond to failures. It's all rags to riches or somebody's new tech invention that made it big. Very few people are willing to talk about when they've faced defeat."

"Now you're getting it! They sure don't. It's all pie in the sky, but that's not reality. What about the twenty percent of new businesses that fail in their first year? What do you say to them and the billions of dollars they've lost? Should they give up? Or is a better solution to get back up and try again?"

For the next twenty-five minutes, the passionate conversation continued. Miguel chimed in about his first venture in the States selling knock-off handbags—which almost got him deported. Luke offered more details about CataSail's unraveling and how his family invented crazy ways to dodge the press who camped outside of their home. Luke couldn't help but find himself deeply engaged as the men laughed and enjoyed another cup of coffee. Who wouldn't be comfortable with these men who seemed so authentic and raw? Like a breath of fresh air, they spoke intelligently, but with profound humility and wisdom. Luke wasn't even drunk or buzzed, but just being in their presence helped him feel better. Though he didn't want their time together to end, Miguel stood up and grabbed Luke's bag, showing it was time to go.

As the men headed down the elevator and towards the limo parked outside, Luke learned his next destination would be Seattle. However, for this time, he'd be flying solo. Miguel assured him that every detail was taken care of and that a car would be waiting to take him to his next host. Confident that his guides had everything planned out, the men shook hands and said goodbye.

Within a few minutes, Luke was quietly seated in the limousine and headed toward Teterboro. Looking out his window, Luke soaked in the sights and sounds of New York's rush hour traffic. Today was like every day in the city that never slept. Alive and at work, its people stirred to their destinations. Pedestrians flooded the sidewalks as they made their way to overcrowded subway stations. Others took to the streets, riding their bikes and electric scooters. Those daring enough to drive took great pleasure in honking their horns at slow movers. Luke chuckled at the beautiful chaos. The city was moving on. It didn't care about his past or failures. And with the exception of four investors living in Manhattan, it wasn't offended by his profit and loss or balance sheet.

A few days ago, things seemed so different. Luke was ashamed of CataSail's demise. It was an ugly scar, meant to be hidden from public sight. However, after his conversations with Aaron, AJ, and Miguel, he now felt less ashamed of his hardship. Sure, Luke had faced some hard times, but that didn't mean he was done fighting. Though his morning started in anger, principle two was starting to make sense. Opening his phone, Luke's fingers began typing a response for his investors.

Thanks, Mike. I'll call you on Monday afternoon when I get back in town. The way I see it, we've got nothing to lose by having a quick chat. I'm sure we can figure out something together that's a win-win.

10 A DOC WITH A VISION

Luke climbed on board, stopping briefly to greet the pilot who sat comfortably in the cockpit. Passing through the galley, the copilot handed him a packed lunch for the trip. Thankful he wouldn't go hungry on the flight, he sat down in one of the leather chairs facing the rear of the plane. Though uncertain where in Seattle they were headed, he felt delighted to be visiting the city, as Luke loved the unique architecture and numerous coffee shops. Lifting off, Luke yawned to pop his ears and hit the recline button to lean back in his seat.

For the first time on his journey, he sat alone with his thoughts. The last two days had been a blur, and more than anything, he desired some space to process. Closing his eyes, Luke took a deep breath and then slowly released the air to focus. The contest, or whatever Stanton wanted to call it, was quite unusual and not at all what he had expected. To his surprise, no rules documented how one wins, and the contestants were isolated from each other. AJ, though polite and knowledgeable about business, seemed to be an unpolished country bumpkin. In contrast, Miguel didn't speak about business. Instead, he was always grinning and overflowing with unbridled optimism. And then there were his two hosts—a missionary talking about having a mission and an amputee telling him to overcome. Luke chuckled to himself as he considered the insanity of it all. Had he not been sitting on the plane, he wouldn't have believed any of it.

Extending his footrest, he continued to ponder his situation. The contest was a creative idea, and admittedly, he probably would never have come on the trip without its intrigue. Of course, the whole thing was corporate headhunting in disguise, but how could they justify spending millions of dollars in prize money? More absurd was the enormous expense of flying him across the globe for these brief and seemingly insignificant meetings. Then again, if Stanton Enterprises was a multibillion-dollar operation, maybe they knew more about recruiting than anyone.

As he continued to think, Luke remembered AJ's words from his first night. Previously, Luke was under the impression that the contestants were only competing for prize money. At the time, he disregarded its value because of JROB Holdings' lawsuit. However, now that he realized the winner became the CEO at one of Stanton's companies, the idea began to fascinate him. What if he somehow won the contest? For the next several minutes, Luke thought about the possibilities and how great it would be to have a fresh start. Even if he lost everything, his new position and salary would easily allow him to start over again. But what business was he being considered for? And what were his chances of winning? Resolving that it would be impossible to figure everything out, Luke decided to let it all go and just enjoy himself by watching movies until they reached Seattle.

As they started their final descent, Luke ate his lunch. Shortly thereafter, they touched down at Boeing Field, a smaller airport about six miles south of downtown Seattle. Directed by the pilots, Luke headed inside the private terminal and let them know he was a contestant with Stanton Enterprises. As suggested, the woman at the desk handled everything and picked up the phone to confirm Luke's transportation. Within two minutes, a white stretch limo appeared, and Luke was off to meet his next host. After a ten-minute drive on Interstate 5, the car took exit 167 towards East Lake Avenue and onto Aloha Street. Finally, they pulled into the circular drop-off where the limo driver parked and exited the vehicle. Opening Luke's door, he handed him a folded sheet of paper with printed text that read: *Take the elevator to the second floor. Look for "Red Brick Bistro" signs. Be seated and Dr. Torres will find you soon.*

As Luke exited the vehicle, a large yellow banner draped against the tall brick building caught his attention. It read: *Where state of the art meets the art of compassion.* A moment of heaviness fell over him as he connected the dots and became aware of his location. Entering the building, he spotted two women in wheelchairs waiting for their transportation, their heads round and smooth, a sure sign they'd been receiving chemotherapy. Luke smiled at them brightly and then proceeded toward the elevators and to the second floor. Entering the cafe, he sat down at a table to await his host.

Within ten minutes, a tallish woman dressed in a white lab coat, pink slacks, and running shoes walked towards him smiling. To Luke's surprise, she wasn't Hispanic as her name suggested. Instead, she was a fair-skinned woman in her late fifties or early sixties with a pretty smile and short blondish-gray hair.

Extending her hand to introduce herself, she said, "Luke Voightmann, I presume?"

"That's me."

"I'm Dr. Torres. Could I join you?"

Luke stood up and extended his hand in return, saying, "Yes, ma'am. It's nice to meet you. I guess my shirt helped you find me?"

The woman nodded as she sat down, saying, "Yes, that was Miguel's idea. The shirts make it easier for me to find everyone."

After a few pleasantries, Dr. Torres was ready to begin. Pulling out her paper index cards and putting on her glasses, she said, "Well, I believe you know how this goes. Unfortunately, I have a pretty tight schedule today, so I won't be able to spend too much time with you. Do you have any questions before we get started?"

Though her face was kind and her words neutral, Luke's host seemed extremely focused and short on time, causing Luke to feel slightly unsure of himself. Uncertain of how he would relate to a female oncologist, he cleared his throat and said, "I don't think so."

Before speaking, Dr. Torres looked intensively down at her watch as if to set a starting point. "So, could you start by telling me what you wanted to be when you grew up? In other words, when you were a child, what did you dream about doing as an adult?"

Luke thought for a second before responding. "Well, it's kind of corny, but I wanted to swim with the whales at Sea World. So, I'd say my dream was to become a marine biologist."

Dr. Torres laughed as she said, "Swimming with Shamu, huh? That sounds kind of fun—and slightly dangerous. Any other childhood dreams?"

"Well, for a season I wanted to play professional baseball. Then I thought about becoming a criminal prosecutor. But when I sat on the bench in little league and realized that prosecutors don't get paid much, those ideas didn't last long. At MIT, the entrepreneurial bug hit me, and I realized I could make money and be my own boss. That's when I dove in. I think I was a late bloomer with knowing what I wanted to do in life."

Dr. Torres nodded in agreement. "It's hard when you're a kid and struggling to figure out what's next. That's helpful though. I asked about your childhood dreams because sometimes people end up doing what they envisioned as a child. Since you didn't start thinking about entrepreneurship until college, let's talk about the vision for your yacht company and how you came up with that. What got you interested in building boats?"

"I'd have to say it was my partner, Dellin. We met in college, and he was the one with the boating background," Luke said, curious about why it mattered.

"Okay, that's helpful," the doctor responded. "You're doing fine, Luke, but let's talk about the vision of the company. Who came up with the idea to build these high-tech catamarans?"

"Well, we both kind of did—that is, my partner and me. We designed the first model together in our senior year. But once we got started, I just focused on business development."

"So after the first boat, you weren't involved with the creation of your products?" the doctor said curiously.

Luke shifted slightly in his seat. "Boat designing wasn't really my strength, so Dellin and the design team created our later models. I was the CEO and Dellin was our COO, sort of like a partnership, I guess you could say. I was involved in the process, I just didn't create the designs."

"Okay, that makes sense," Dr. Torres nodded as she looked down at her note cards. "In case you're wondering, I'm trying to understand the inner workings of the company and how it reached maturity. I see here you guys were on the Inc. 5000 list for a season. We find that usually there's someone or something driving vision when a company experiences hyper-growth. In your business, how were you able to grow so quickly? Do you think it was because the boats were revolutionary?"

Luke scratched his head as he thought about the doctor's words. After thinking for a few seconds, he continued, "Our boats were cutting edge, that's for sure. They were the best catamaran yachts in the world, but that was only part of our success. To answer your question about how we grew so quickly, I'd have to say it was a total team effort. We had some great people all working together. Hitting the Inc. 5000 list was nice and all, but we busted our tails to get there."

"Hmmm," the doctor responded. "I understand teamwork, but I'm interested in who or what was driving you guys forward. Having a great team is critical for success, but a great team will only follow a leader with a vision. If your partner and his team were building your main product, then what specifically were you doing for the company to make it grow?"

"I did everything—I was the CEO," Luke responded quickly. After taking a breath, he continued his answer to explain himself. "I don't know what you know about business or leading a start-up, but when you're trying to grow, you do just about everything. I hired staff, sold boats, led marketing teams, expanded operations, and raised capital, among dozens of other things."

Dr. Torres listened patiently, but it was clear she wasn't quite satisfied with Luke's answer. Squinting her eyes and wrinkling her forehead, she continued calmly. "I'm sure you all worked very hard. Please understand that I'm not here to judge your performance. I'm looking for something specific. Help me understand because something isn't quite adding up here. From what you've told me, I've learned you were not a major part of the boat building or design process. In other words, the vision for your product was guided by your partner. You then told me that the hyper-growth wasn't because of the boats but because of a team effort. When I asked you what you did specifically as CEO, you basically said 'everything.' It kind of sounds like your company grew by chance or luck. While this is possible, it's highly unlikely, as usually there's someone directly responsible for a company's success. What I need to know is who fed the vision for the company. Who drove the growth? Point blank question—was that you or someone else?"

Though feeling a little annoyed at how she had depicted him as an apathetic leader, Luke didn't hesitate with his response, saying confidently, "I was the CEO. It was me."

Dr. Torres nodded and continued. "Okay, I know these questions might seem different, but they are important for me to know what or who instigated the growth. So, one last time, just to be clear—you were the one who guided the vision for the company? It wasn't your partner, investors, or anyone else, correct? You were the driver?"

Again, Luke confirmed his answer confidently, with a slight hint of dissatisfaction. "It was me. As CEO, it was my job to push us forward. Obviously, I tried to listen to input from everyone on our executive team, but at the end of the day, I was in charge of everything, especially driving our vision."

Dr. Torres removed her glasses and placed them along with her notecards into one of her lab coat pockets. Seeming to be content with Luke's answer, she sat back and spoke slowly to explain herself. "Let me

A Doc with a Vision

share with you my role in the contest. I'm here today to see if you're a visionary thinker. We all know you're driven, but what we're interested in is your vision skills. Our statement might help everything make sense to you. **The *EntreSpirit* has VISION. It consistently thinks and daydreams about the future. It takes what seems invisible to others and turns it into reality.**" Like everyone else, she spoke the special statement from memory in an almost robotic fashion.

"Daydreams about the future, huh?" Luke said out loud without thinking. He didn't intend for it to come out so contrary, but it was too late—the words had already left his mouth.

"Yes, daydreaming. Is there something wrong with that?" the doctor asked.

"No, not really, I guess. I just don't know too many CEOs who have time to sit around daydreaming."

Unmoved, Dr. Torres took a breath and then responded. "You can call it daydreaming, brainstorming, vision planning, creative thinking, or whatever you want. It's all the same. The *EntreSpirit* is always thinking."

Dr. Torres paused for a moment, her hand on her chin. "Let me see if I can explain this another way. Since you're from Florida, I imagine you've been to Disney World."

"Yes, plenty of times," Luke confirmed.

"Okay, great. This will help you understand a little bit better. You might already know this, but the idea for the Magic Kingdom came to Walt Disney one day when he was sitting on a park bench eating peanuts. He was watching his little girls play and thought about how great it would be if there was a new kind of park where parents and children could all play together. I imagine it was just another thought, but it was the start of something much bigger. It was the seed for everything Disney has become today."

Dr. Torres paused again. Smiling, she seemed to be thinking about something delightful, and said, "Let me share a story with you. I'm giving away my age here, but when I was eight years old, my parents took us to Disneyland down in Anaheim. This is well before the park was open in Florida, but I do remember that day vividly. As I walked down Main Street holding my dad's hand, I realized how proud he was to be able to bring us there. He seemed to know everything about the park, almost as if he was more excited than I was. We visited the castle, rode the monorail, and took the Skyway across the different lands. I sang 'It's a Small World After All' for weeks afterward. We watched a parade, and before we left, my dad bought me cotton candy and a shiny red balloon."

Lost in her fond memory, the doctor continued to smile, her light blue eyes staring off into the distance. For five seconds, she didn't say a word. Before it became too awkward, she looked up and spoke. "That is one of my favorite memories of all time, and you know why I have that memory? Because Walt Disney's vision was to build a place where families could play together."

Luke smiled at Dr. Torres, who now seemed to be a little warmer. Acknowledging her story, he said, "My parents took us a few times too. Those are great memories."

"Yes, they are," Dr. Torres confirmed. "So, let me explain why I just told you that story. If you truly have the *EntreSpirit*, I would bet that you already have more creative thoughts than you could act on in one hundred lifetimes. You're probably always coming up with new ideas. Walt Disney didn't just have an idea though. He took it to the next level and stirred up a clear vision inside of him. Day and night for years and years, he kept daydreaming. It started small as the first plan for Disneyland was an eight-acre stretch of land called Mickey Mouse Park. He didn't stop there though. Disney kept dreaming. He visited other theme parks. More than his films, he was all consumed with his amusement park idea. Finally, after years of planning and research, Disneyland opened in 1954, but not on an eight-acre parcel. Instead, it was one hundred and sixty acres. That was back then, but stop and think about the Disney empire today. They have cruises, resorts, movies, and have become an incredibly profitable, successful, and powerful corporation. Why? I believe it all goes back to Walt's creative vision and his ability to continually keep it in front of him."

Though Luke enjoyed listening to his host's business stories, something inside of him didn't quite understand where she was going. Trying not to sound negative, he said, "I understand what you're saying. As you mentioned, I've had so many ideas through the years, and I think Disney is a great example of imagination. I also agree with setting a vision as it guides the course for the future. I guess where I'm struggling is the part about daydreaming. To be honest, it seems kind of fluffy, and I wonder how many executives really have time for that."

Dr. Torres offered a small chuckle and then said passionately, "Right? In our busy world, nobody has time for dreaming. Instead, we're too busy working on things that aren't important. I believe that most people don't lack vision or ideas. No, we have an abundance of those. What we lack is clarity! And because we don't have clarity, we continue to work on things that don't matter so that we look busy. Why daydreaming is so important is because it gives incredible clarity and specific details to our vision. In other words, this creative thinking process gives us handles. It allows us to wrap our minds around the whole vision and see it! One of my favorite Walt Disney quotes is, 'First, think. Second, dream. Third, believe. And finally, dare.'"

"That's an interesting quote," Luke said casually, now feeling more comfortable with his host. "Can I ask you a question though?"

"Sure. Go right ahead," Dr. Torres responded, encouraged by Luke's desire to learn.

"You're talking to me about vision and daydreaming, but you're a doctor. I've met a lot of doctors in my life, and none of them seem to have time for anything. They are some of the busiest people I've ever met. Even before we got started today, you said you didn't have long to spend with me. So, how do you have this abundance of time to daydream with your schedule?"

"Ah, now we are getting somewhere. Let me explain something first and then I'll tell you my story. You see, we believe that most people have some sort of vision for their life. The problem is that their vision is often unclear. The reason it's unclear is that they haven't spent enough time thinking through or daydreaming through all the details. The only thing worse than an unclear vision is a stale vision. It became stale because they didn't keep it in front of them. They got too busy and stopped daydreaming a long time ago and found themselves neck-deep in work. Because of all this work, they don't have time to think through their vision. Because they don't think through their vision, they continue to do trivial work. It becomes a crazy cycle where they're living, but they're not living out the vision for their lives. Does that make any sense?"

Luke nodded as he listened. Becoming more vulnerable, he said, "It does. So, you're basically saying that because people don't make time to daydream, their vision is unclear. And because it is unclear, they're doing things that don't really matter. I think everyone struggles with this. You become so busy working on stuff that you don't even know why you're doing it anymore. It's hard when you're a CEO because there are so many responsibilities and people pulling on you."

Dr. Torres smiled and said, "It's not just CEOs. The crazy cycle can happen to everyone, including doctors. You see, when I finished medical school, I couldn't wait to help women fight breast cancer. It was something I deeply cared about, and so I worked, and I worked, and I worked. I was doing an incredibly good thing and helping save my patients' lives. However, I became increasingly aware of another problem. I was working so much that it left little room for anything else in my life. As a doctor, I wanted to start a nonprofit to help women afford cancer treatments. I wanted to research so that maybe we could find a cure, but with all of my patients, there wasn't much time for that. When I got married, my vision expanded. I wanted to be a good wife and mother. We all want more for our lives, but we're often so busy doing our work that we aren't able to stop long enough to really think through the details and prioritize what matters most."

Luke nodded. Thinking about his work habits, he said, "I'm guilty of that too. Sometimes, my days would just fly by. I was putting out fires everywhere. By the time I left the office, I felt like I hadn't accomplished anything meaningful at all."

"That's how it goes," the doctor said softly. "The squeaky wheel gets the oil. It's easy to fall into that rut, and once you're there, it's really hard to climb out."

"Agreed," Luke added. "So, you believe the solution is to just daydream a little more?"

"Yes. It might sound different, but we believe the most successful visionaries are intentional about dreaming. Do you know why they have me talking to you about this today?"

"No, but I imagine you're going to tell me," Luke answered with a smile.

"Six years ago, I was asked to be a part of these contests. At first, I couldn't understand why they'd ask me. First of all, I'm a doctor, not an entrepreneur. I've never been a CEO and don't care to be. So, I said, 'why do you want me to talk about vision?' Their response changed my paradigm."

"What did they tell you?" Luke asked genuinely.

"They told me that CEOs could learn a lot from how I manage myself. You see, when I started out as a doctor, I quickly realized I had more patients than I could see. I had more phone calls to return than I had time. There were more trivial tasks than I could complete. Medical school teaches you a lot of things, but it doesn't teach you how to manage yourself. I tried to keep up, but it was never-ending. I was twenty-seven years old, trying to balance my career, my patients, my marriage, and a six-month-old baby. Outwardly, I looked like I had it together. But inside, I was drowning and felt completely overwhelmed. I had big dreams for our nonprofit and for finding a cure, but my vision was fading fast. Almost like a candle, my dreams were getting snuffed out because I couldn't keep up. I imagine as a successful CEO, you can relate to feeling overwhelmed like this."

"Absolutely," Luke said softly to his host, who seemed to be transforming in front of his very eyes. She was no longer a medical doctor—cold and clinical. Instead, she was human, a warm and caring woman, trying to balance the burdens of her family and career. Any walls Luke had built up were quickly falling as she spoke humbly about her struggles.

"Well, then you know how hard it is to juggle when there are too many balls in the air. I knew that if I didn't slow down, some of the balls were going to come crashing down. I decided I needed to take a few steps back, at least for a season. Instead of trying to do more and work harder, I did less. I cut my hours. I saw fewer patients. Even at home, we did everything we could to simplify our lives. That's the first time I realized the power of doing less and daydreaming. Because I had more time to think, I became more clear about my vision and objectives. I was a better mom, wife, and doctor simply because I had enough margin to think. Because I was willing to stop long enough to think back then, we've been able to do so much today. We've helped thousands of women with our non-profit, I'm still seeing patients, we're pursuing a cure, and my family is in balance. Not because I did more, but because I did less and daydreamed."

"I agree with what you're saying on a personal level," Luke confirmed. "But I think the world of business is a little different. Less isn't more. More is more, and there is unbelievable pressure to achieve results."

"With all due respect, Luke, you're wrong," Dr. Torres responded softly. "Shareholders don't care about how many hours a CEO works. They care about the results of the company. I'm not saying we should be less effective or less profitable, I'm saying we should be more focused. In other words, doing the right things with the time we have. Wouldn't you agree with that?"

Luke hesitated briefly, and then said, "Yes, I understand what you're saying. It's just—well there's a tremendous amount of pressure in the business world is all I'm saying. Especially when you don't know what to do."

Dr. Torres smiled. "That's why you need a clear vision. It's not easy, and you'll have to fight for it. Thinking and dreaming take time, which is something none of us have. To create margin, you won't be able to comply with everyone's requests. You can no longer fill your schedule with meaningless tasks, meetings, and busywork. You'll have to cut the unimportant, simplify your life, and say 'no' to a lot of people. It feels uncomfortable for busy people to sit and dream—but the payoff is huge!

When you do work, you'll have clarity on what you're working on and why you're working on it. Your vision will come alive again and it will be relevant and fresh."

Luke slowly nodded, acknowledging that he was processing her words. "You bring up some valid points, and I'm sure I could have carved out more time for my vision. But this daydreaming thing—or whatever you want to call it—how much time are we talking about?"

"It depends. The greater the vision, the more time it will take. I try to spend at least twenty minutes every day thinking about my vision and planning out my schedule. I know some leaders who spend more and some who spend less. Some do it weekly and others do it monthly. It will be different for you and every visionary, but we believe that anyone who wants to keep their vision relevant must set aside time to daydream about it."

Interrupted by her cellphone chiming from her coat pocket, Dr. Torres removed her device to read a new text message. "Ah, Luke, I'm sorry but I have to be going. I can tell you're a bright young man and have a great future in front of you."

Luke stood up, shook the doctor's hand, and said, "I know you've got a busy schedule and lots of patients to see, but I appreciate your time today."

Dr. Torres, who was now also standing, smiled. "Actually, I've been here since five o'clock this morning, and I'm happy to say I'm headed home. Part of my vision is to spend time with my family. I've got to finish packing because we're headed out for a week of a much-needed vacation. But before I go, let me leave you with one last bit of encouragement. I know you've been through some hard times, so this might help. It's what I tell my patients when their prognosis is good, and I think it applies nicely to your situation."

After pausing briefly, Dr. Torres looked deeply into Luke's eyes, and said, "You're going to make it. Your story isn't over yet. It won't be easy. The truth is, this journey can be painful. And yes, some days you'll be so sick that you want to die, but you can't give up! No matter what, never give up! It might be the hardest thing you've ever done, but you, Luke Voightmann, are going to make it."

Luke exhaled as he digested his host's emotional words. Surprised by her open encouragement, he struggled to form a response. "Thank you. That means more than you realize."

As the doctor left, Luke sank back into his chair. Shaking his head, he chuckled, wondering what he had gotten himself into. Dr. Torres was kind enough, but she was a doctor, so why did Stanton have her talking about having a vision? Who could be next—a bongo player in Mexico talking about finance? None of it made much sense, and Luke, though enjoying himself, couldn't help but wonder what Stanton was doing with the contest. Whatever it was, it sure wasn't normal. One good thing had come from it though. Luke's trip and many conversations had distracted him from the accident and all his sorrow. The pain was still there, but at least it didn't feel as fresh.

Thankful for the reprieve, Luke looked outside the window across from where he was seated. He hoped the weather might cooperate for a walk in the city. It was overcast, but at least it wasn't raining. Standing up and continuing to inspect the weather, he caught a glimpse of himself in the window. His reflection made him pause as he continued staring at his face. Three seconds later, he laughed so loudly that the lady sitting next to him began to look out the window to see what was so funny. With two hours left before his limo returned, Luke left the hospital, knowing exactly where he wanted to go.

11 IT'S A LONG WAY TO CANADA

"Well, look at what we have here. I believe we got ourselves a new passenger!" AJ said as Luke walked down the aisle of the plane. "You look like a whole new man."

Luke smiled, approaching Miguel and AJ, who sat at the mid-cabin conference table. "I decided that I needed a change," Luke said, while rubbing his hand across his now clean-shaven face. "I sure had a hard time flagging down the limo driver though. He didn't recognize me at all."

Miguel stood up and inspected Luke's appearance, now altered by a fresh barbershop shave and haircut, and said, "Mr. Luke, you look good, sir—you look much younger."

"I agree," AJ added, admiring Luke's transformation.

Luke, feeling more confident in his appearance, said, "Thank you, gentlemen. My wife's going to be happy too. She's been begging me to cut off my beard for months."

The men laughed a little as Luke sat down across from AJ, and Miguel headed towards the galley.

"When did you guys get in?" Luke asked.

"Maybe thirty minutes ago. It's been a busy day for us, but I wanted to connect with you before your last two meetings. After tonight, I won't see you again until Friday when we head back to Dallas."

"Should I assume that's when I'll be meeting Stanton?"

AJ nodded as he continued. "That you will, my boy. If all goes as planned, you'll get better acquainted on Friday evening. Tonight, we're off to Canada. Hopefully, you'll get a good night's rest and sleep in a little before you meet your next host tomorrow. Then you'll make your way to North Carolina for your last host on Friday morning. I expect you'll be finished by early afternoon, and then we'll pick you up and head to Dallas. I don't know the plans for Saturday just yet, but you should be home by Sunday afternoon. Does that sound all right with you?"

"Sounds good, sir. You guys seem to have everything organized and it's been pretty seamless," Luke confirmed, appreciative that AJ provided so many details. "I don't know if now is a good time or not, but do you mind if I ask you a few questions before we take off? I'm curious about a few things."

"That's why I'm here. Go right ahead."

Luke took a breath and then slowly exhaled as he thought of the best way to explain what he was thinking. "Well, for starters, this *EntreSpirit* thing. I'm curious why it matters so much?" Luke asked directly.

AJ thought for a second and then said, "Okay, that's a fair question and it goes back to our values. We believe that the biggest asset or advantage our companies will have is their people. We take the stance that human capital is more valuable than anything else, including money. So, to value the *EntreSpirit*, an organization must first believe that its success is directly tied to its people. You tracking with me?"

Luke nodded.

AJ continued, "So why does the *EntreSpirit* matter to us? That's simple. When you're growing a company, you need people who can get things done. The *EntreSpirit* starts things from scratch and builds everything from the ground up. We want self-starters, not people who need handholding and coddling. We're not hiring managers to sustain an existing organization. We won't be micromanaging them or giving them a thick manual to guide them. Instead, they are the ones who will build the systems and write the manuals for others to follow."

AJ's words made sense. Though Luke didn't understand his various hosts' personalities, he didn't have trouble following AJ, who seemed to be an expert at the *EntreSpirit*. As he thought through AJ's words, another line of questions flowed into Luke's mind, and he said, "I think I understand, and honestly, I agree with a lot of what you're saying, but how do you find these self-starters? It seems that most companies hire from within or based upon the applicant's resume. What about their experience? None of your hosts have asked me anything about my past."

Sounding extremely sure of himself, AJ addressed Luke's questions. "In most cases, we do promote and hire from within, but this contest is a little different. You'll learn more about that this weekend if you're selected. However, I'll tell you plain as day that we don't care about your resume, alma mater, or any of that bull. All that stuff ain't what it used to be anyway. What matters to us is one thing—the *EntreSpirit*."

AJ's abundance of confidence, poor grammar, and contrary beliefs caused Luke to feel slightly uncomfortable. Luke wasn't trying to be disagreeable, but he didn't understand and asked, "You guys don't care about resumes or education?"

AJ smiled, not offended that Luke didn't seem to grasp everything. Continuing confidently, he said, "To us, a resume is nothing more than a bunch of information that someone wants us to see. But that ain't the real person. It won't tell us if they've got what it takes to grow a company. Now, I'm sure someone on our team scoped you out, but I'm doubtful they've looked at your resume. Most guys like yourself aren't exactly passing them out. Am I right?"

"No—I mean, no, I don't have a resume," Luke said, now hesitating. "I've been an entrepreneur for fifteen years, so I've never really needed one."

"Exactly! That's my point, young man!" AJ responded passionately, hoping Luke would see his angle. "You don't have a resume. If you did, what would it show for experience? That you've worked a single job for your entire life? Now, let's send you out job hunting. Put you up against a mid-level manager with a polished resume, MBA, and twelve years of corporate experience. And guess what? He'd probably be the one who gets the job—not you! But who is more qualified to start something from scratch and make it grow? An entrepreneur, or the guy with the polished resume? I'm gonna tell you right now it ain't the corporate suit! I know that! You know that!"

Though Luke didn't buy into everything AJ said, he did agree that his entrepreneurial background was valuable. His curiosity continued as he thought about hiring. "What about people with bad character or lack of integrity? Doesn't the *EntreSpirit* care about any of that?"

"Of course!" AJ answered. "There are some red flags that we look out for when we hold contests or hire people. This will sound overly simplistic, but in most cases, we find that if our people support all five *EntreSpirit* principles, they will be great leaders for our organization. I know it is a lot to take in, but I think this will all make sense by the end of the week when you understand the contest a little more and why we've brought you here."

Luke listened intently as he rubbed his fingers across his clean-shaven chin. Continuing, he said, "I hope you know I'm not complaining, sir. I'm just trying to wrap my head around everything. Over the last fifteen years, I've met a lot of high-level executives who were interested in buying our boats. I'd bet that the vast majority of them couldn't have cared less about their organization's mission. They were smart, but not what you guys would describe as overcomers. If they had setbacks, they surely didn't talk about it. If anything, they blamed their failures on others. Honestly, if I talked to them about daydreaming for their vision, they would have laughed in my face. This is just a much different approach."

"Attaboy!" AJ said to encourage Luke. "Now you're starting to see it. That's the *EntreSpirit*! It's not business as usual, and believe me, that's a good thing! Do you know how rare it is for a CEO to be passionate about their product these days? Many lead purely for their own ego and wouldn't know what a mission was if it slapped them in the face. Instead, they sit around trying to look good. And what about overcoming? How many executives have faced what you are going through? I'm talking about hard times! They're complaining if they can't get a manicure every week. They ain't tough and have probably never been in a fistfight in their lives. And how many executives carve out time to think through their vision? The truth is, most of them say they can't because they're too busy. If they slowed down and actually hired people with—"

Before AJ could finish his rant, the plane chimed, indicating the engines were starting and they would soon be taking off. AJ paused to peek outside his window just as Miguel returned to the table to address him.

"Excuse me, sir. I spoke to him. It's not good news. Would you like to discuss this in private?"

AJ nodded and waved to Miguel to go back to the front of the plane and then said to Luke, "I'm sorry, but would you excuse me for a minute? Miguel and I were waiting on a call, and I need to address this with him."

Within a few minutes, AJ returned to his seat and was ready to continue the conversation.

"Everything is okay, I hope," Luke said sincerely.

"Yes, it's fine. Miguel just got the news that one of our previous winners is backing out, and so he wanted me to know. He took it kind of hard because he really liked this fella, and he was one of our sharpest winners."

Luke's curiosity wouldn't rest until he knew why the contestant had given up. "Oh, I'm sorry to hear that. Why is he backing out?" he said as nonchalantly as possible.

Unbothered by the question, AJ added, "It happens once in a while, and it's part of what we do. Some birds aren't meant to be caged, I guess. You have to realize that when you add people with the *EntreSpirit*, you're bringing on someone with a lot of potential, and they can pretty much do whatever they want with their lives. It's nothing for them to go out on their own and start another company. We want them to partner with us and do everything we can to entice them. However, sometimes they see the opportunity as a cage. But I'm getting ahead of myself, Luke. You don't need to worry about any of that stuff unless we make you an offer. Let's get back to what you were talking about before. Do you mind if we get comfortable before we take off? We've all had a long day and I want to stretch out my legs."

As the plane started to taxi towards the runway, AJ headed to the cabin directly behind the conference table. Luke followed, and both men made themselves comfortable on the leather sofas facing each other. Previously, the space had been Luke's bedroom, but the couches now served as a comfortable spot for the men to relax. AJ waved to Miguel, who seemed to read his mind, and quickly brought the men two full glasses of white wine. Miguel left the men and then returned—but this time, he carried a metal bucket with an unopened bottle and a full glass of wine poured for himself. Sitting down on the couch beside AJ, he secured the bucket between his feet.

"Luke, are you missing your family, sir? Are they doing okay without you home?" Miguel said as he took a small sip of his wine.

"They're doing fine. I miss them, but we were able to catch up last night, so that was nice. How about you guys? How does your family handle it when you're away?"

Miguel spoke first. "My wife and I talk every night on video when I am gone. My two sons moved out of our house now. One's at college in Houston and another son is married with a new baby boy. Since my grandson come, my wife doesn't miss me anymore. She spends all her time being grandma."

"Ain't that the truth," AJ added. "We've got five kids and fourteen grandchildren to date. My wife is always with one of them, and she usually goes for a visit when I'm traveling."

"So, you guys have to travel a lot for work?" Luke asked, interested to bring the conversation back to the contest.

This time, AJ spoke first. "We only do contests a few times each year.

So, we're gone for maybe, six to eight weeks at the most, which isn't too bad. It's just enough to keep us busy."

As the plane approached the runway and began to power up, AJ encouraged the men to drink up, so their full wine glasses wouldn't spill. After each of them happily enjoyed a few large sips, the plane was in the air, and Luke was determined to continue his questioning. Before he had a chance, AJ asked him a question instead.

"Tell us about Dr. Torres. How was your meeting with her today?"

"Well, it wasn't as dramatic as flying in a helicopter over the Amazon, but I've got to say that I really liked her," Luke answered as he thought back through the conversation.

AJ smiled as he continued, now saying the statement for principle three. "**The *EntreSpirit* has VISION. It consistently thinks and daydreams about the future. It takes what seems invisible to others and turns it into reality.** I've yet to meet a contestant that didn't learn a lot from the good doctor."

"What do you think about daydreaming, Mr. Luke? You hear of this idea before? Were you a daydreamer at your boat company?" Miguel asked.

"Well, I'll admit I haven't been much of a dreamer, but I think I might start doing some of that. The doctor made a great case for it. I've always thought of myself as a visionary, but after talking to Dr. Torres, I feel like she pegged me pretty well. I got so busy doing my work that I didn't have time to feed my vision or think through the details. I don't understand everything she said, but I do see how having margin to think would be important for a leader," Luke answered and then took another large sip from his glass, finishing it off.

"Sounds like she made an impact. These are good lessons," AJ said in an encouraging voice.

Luke nodded and said, "It is interesting for sure and got me thinking. I have another question though. If creating space to think and dream is so important for your vision, why aren't leaders more intentional about it?"

AJ didn't hesitate before responding, "Well, there are a lot of reasons, but these are the big two. First of all, most executives would likely say it isn't very productive to sit quietly and allow themselves to think. They've never done it before, so they get distracted by an email, text, or phone call. Secondly, very few executives or teams have enough margin in their schedules to allow them to do so. In most organizations, there are more objectives than time. When that happens, the vision is neglected and traded for tasks. If it happens for too long, the vision gets muddy and people don't even know what they're doing or why they're doing it anymore. This happens all the time in larger companies."

"Well, we weren't that big, but I feel like I can relate. Especially when we were growing so fast. I'd come in early and stay late. I busted my tail working all day long. Still, everywhere I looked, there were tons of things that needed addressing. I didn't have time though. Nobody did. We created a complex business where we had so much work to do, but we didn't know where we were going or why we were doing all this busywork."

As Luke thought about CataSail, he remembered the chaos and continual stress. AJ could see the regret on Luke's face, and he spoke up to encourage him. "It's not easy, young man. You tasted success, and the natural instinct is to work harder to keep growing. The demands to keep up become too great, and before you know it, there is no time for your vision."

"Ugh, that was us," Luke said with disgust. "We were growing by some 200 percent. From the outside, we looked polished and professional, but inwardly, we were quite a mess. I didn't have a clear vision for where we were going, and I didn't take time to think about it. I just pushed my staff for better marketing, more boats, and higher revenues. I wanted to build our brand-new headquarters. I wanted new technology and demanded new boat designs. I was so engrossed that I—"

Luke's words faded as he pondered what he had just said. It was an emotional moment for him as he came face to face with his own actions. Acknowledging that he was the one who always demanded more was painful as he thought back to his staff meetings and how his leaders would tell him they needed to slow down. They needed margin to catch up and to work on the business, not just in the business.

Both Miguel and AJ were silent for a moment, giving Luke plenty of space to think. Finally, AJ said, in a gentle tone, "Your company grew because you're an entrepreneur. That's who you are and that's what led us to you."

Luke lifted his head and smiled. "I'm all right. I'm just starting to see things in a different light. I do have a serious question though. This one is for Miguel. Are you going to open up that other bottle of wine, or am I going to look at this empty glass all night?" Luke's humor caused AJ to laugh as Miguel jumped up to open the bottle.

"Yes, sir, Mr. Luke. Coming right up!" Miguel said, also laughing.

As Miguel refilled the men's glasses, Luke became serious once again. "AJ, there's something I don't quite understand with principle three. We've talked about creating time to renew the vision, be it daydreaming, thinking, or meditating, but I was buried in work. Practically speaking, how could I have dug out from that? For that matter, how could any organization dig out from the mess so that they have the margin to focus on their vision?"

AJ leaned forward. "Well, there is a solution, but it's not easy because it takes the leader to initiate it and the whole team to buy into the change. The first step is what I like to call trimming the fat. That's a country boy's words, but you could call it restructuring if you'd like. The leader must eliminate nonessential tasks—meetings, projects, and any new ideas until there is more margin. The entire organization will have to fight off the temptation to fill that void with new ideas. The second step is that every department leader must think through and refresh their vision. They ask their teams for ideas on how they could do things better. Do they need new technology? Do they need more staff? It's an open dialogue about how to improve operations. If the organization gives them enough margin to think and dream introspectively, the vision will become crystal clear. That is the blueprint, but it still has to get done. If the margin is extended, the leaders will be able to implement the vision, which will make the organization more healthy and efficient. What ends up happening is that the organization will be able to do more than ever, while still having the margin to think and dream."

"That makes sense, AJ. Is there more to it than that?" Luke asked sincerely.

AJ took a sip from his glass and then answered, "There is, and that's why we hire people with the *EntreSpirit*. You see, if the CEO creates margin for a team but leads a pack of managers without the *EntreSpirit*, innovation won't happen. Though it might boost morale, it won't make the company better because the managers won't push the envelope. They'll play it safe and simply pass the time. However, if the company employs leaders with the *EntreSpirit*, then things will get done."

As AJ finished speaking, he leaned forward, placing his hands on his knees, and said, "Now, that's enough business talk for one day. What do you boys say we have some supper and relax?"

As the men ate, Luke thought about the irony of his situation. Here he sat, sipping wine and eating a fine meal high above the clouds. For the first time in a long time, he was truly excited to talk about business. Thinking back, he realized it was just seven days ago that he stormed out of his house and moved onto his boat. Now, it seemed like an eternity ago. It could have been the combination of the altitude and the wine on his empty stomach, but Luke felt optimism like he hadn't felt in a long time.

12 AN EDUCATION IN NOVA SCOTIA

Luke didn't expect the hotel alarm clock to be needed, but he had set it just in case, and was now thankful for the beeping sounds that awoke him. Late last night, they landed at Halifax Stanfield, a small private airport in Eastern Nova Scotia. By the time they finished with Canadian customs, rented a car, and arrived at the hotel, it was already 11:30, according to Luke's watch. AJ had left, likely attending to the other contestant, while Miguel and Luke stayed behind to meet their new host.

Heading to the bathroom, Luke caught a glimpse of himself in the mirror, reminding him of his new appearance. He liked seeing his clean-shaven face and short hair again. Flexing and sucking in his gut, he tried to calculate how long it would take to get back in shape. After a quick shower, he dressed in the clothes provided by Miguel for their stay. Today Luke's outfit included khaki cargo pants and a white sweatshirt with a red Canadian maple leaf. Luke smiled as he thought of how ridiculous he looked and decided to snap a picture of himself and send it to his wife.

With ten minutes to kill before lunch, Luke headed to the second room of the suite. Opening the curtains, he discovered quite a boring view of the street below and the office building across from the hotel. Though he'd hoped to see the harbor or Atlantic, at least his room at the

Prince George Hotel was spacious with its separate bedroom and living room. He'd never been to the east coast of Canada and was looking forward to seeing the sights. Luke pulled out his phone, planning to check a map and see where they were located. Instead, a picture of his smiling wife took over the screen as his phone began to vibrate.

"They made you shave? Are you serious?" Meredith cried out in amusement without greeting her husband.

"They didn't make me, I wanted to! I was getting tired of it—and by the way, good morning to you too, honey!" Luke responded sarcastically.

"I'm sorry—good morning! I was just shocked when I saw that picture. Where are you today?"

"You didn't see my sweatshirt? That's the only hint you're getting," Luke said, laughing.

"Canada? Really?"

"Yep! Nova Scotia."

"Awe man! I want to go there! So, how has it been? How are the people treating you? Are you glad you went?"

"It's been good. Really good! I think I needed this trip, babe. I can't explain it, but I needed it. Honestly, I don't know much about the contest yet or if I have a shot at winning, but I'm having a good time. These people are so very different from everyone we know. They're good at business, but it isn't stuffy like you'd think."

For the next few minutes, Luke filled in the missing details from his trip. Starting with Dr. Torres, Luke shared how she explained that he probably wasn't daydreaming enough. Then, he discussed his interesting business talk with AJ and Miguel last night.

"I have so much more to share, but I've got to get going pretty soon. How are you and the boys? Is everyone okay?" Luke added.

"We're doing okay. Everything is pretty quiet here. We're going to my parents' condo on Friday to spend some time with them. The boys are excited about that, but they miss you and can't wait to have their daddy home. Do you know what time you'll be back on Sunday?"

"I'm not sure yet, but I'll let you know as soon as I can."

After the conversation ended, Luke headed to the elevator and down to the lobby to meet Miguel. The men shook hands and sat down at the hotel's restaurant for lunch.

"So, Miguel, tell me about who I'm meeting today!" Luke said genuinely.

"Oh, today is very good for you, sir. You meet our friend Tulo, a very smart businessman. He will teach you how to become a very smart entrepreneur. You will like him very much, I'm sure of it."

Though Luke was curious about why his host was so smart, Luke decided not to pursue the conversation. Regardless of the hosts' true personalities, Miguel was always so positive. After a satisfying lunch, it was time for Luke's meeting. Leaving the concrete city, they headed south on Highway 349. The sleepy two-lane road hugged the coast, void of much traffic. Just as Luke started to feel bored by the drive, sweeping views of the Atlantic opened up, sparking Luke's interest in the people who lived there. The homes seemed simple but strong—able to withstand the fierce northeasters coming off the Atlantic. As the asphalt road ended, a small sign with an arrow spelled out: *Duncan's Cove*.

Miguel continued around the corner and then pointed to where they were going. Rising above the coast, a four-story eclectic white building stood tall and proud. Unlike the typical homes in the area, its towering heights and rectangular shape immediately drew attention. Continuing down the driveway, Luke observed the huge floor-to-ceiling windows that presented spectacular views for those lucky enough to live inside. Though Luke didn't know who lived there, he loved the house already. It was white, modern, and offered magnificent sights of the water, much like his home on Palm Island.

Putting the car into park, Miguel said, "Mr. Luke, please wait here, sir. I go to speak with Mr. Tulo and then you get started."

Luke nodded, and Miguel headed down the walkway, vanishing from sight. For the next few minutes, Luke closed his eyes to think. Reclining in his seat, he wondered who he'd be meeting today. He'd run the gamut with his first three hosts, and the only thing that he was sure about is that he couldn't be sure of anything. While still pondering the contest, Miguel abruptly opened the passenger side door, which startled Luke. As he jolted to life, he started to swear—causing Miguel to roar with laughter. With heart pounding, Luke exited the car when he noticed another man standing behind Miguel.

"Oh, Mr. Luke. I scared you bad, sir. I'm sorry!" Miguel said, pretending to be concerned. "Meet Mr. Tulo—awhit—aski. Um...Mr. Tulo, I never say your name the right way, sir. How do you say it again?"

"It's Tulowitzki!" The man said as he shook hands with Luke. "It's not an easy name, but it's been with me since I was born. You can call me Tulo though...that's what everyone calls me."

Tulo's thick brown hair, dark eyes, and olive skin made him more good-looking than a lot of men in their sixties. The absence of gray hair and the man's slender build added to his youthful appearance. Dressed in a stylish gray suit, with a white shirt, tie, vest, and polished shoes, he looked to be a professional in every way.

"Luke Voightmann. Good to meet you, sir," Luke said, slightly embarrassed about how Miguel had scared him.

"Miguel, we should be done in about an hour, if that is okay with you. Luke, please come inside and we'll get started." Tulo confirmed as he turned towards the walkway.

As Luke passed Miguel, he felt a pat on the shoulder, and a familiar voice said, "I'll be back later Mr. Luke. Don't you worry. You are safe here. No wild monkeys in Canada."

Luke ignored Miguel's comment, and walking towards the pathway, he shot a scowl over his shoulder—followed by a smile—acknowledging he appreciated Miguel's attempt at humor.

It didn't take Luke long to forget Miguel's joking as they made their way through the back door. The home was truly captivating and immediate views of the Atlantic coast came into sight—its deep blue waters drastically contrasted the white walls and furniture.

As his host shut the door, Tulo smiled and said, "Quite a view, huh?"

Luke nodded, saying, "One of the best I've ever seen. You have some house here, sir. It's remarkable. I live on the water too, but it's nothing compared to this. I imagine the view up top is even better."

"Yeah, it is beautiful this time of year," Tulo said as he headed towards the living room.

"Most people don't know this, but this wasn't always a house. During World War II, it was used as a fortified battery, complete with huge guns and an optical range finder to spot the Nazis. You might be in the safest building in Canada as these are eighteen-inch concrete walls. There are even a couple of bunkers on the hiking trails outside. The home has been heavily renovated, but I love that it was used in the war efforts."

"Wow! That's awesome. It looks amazing. Did you buy it because of its history and then redesign it?" Luke asked as they stood looking out the twenty-foot wall of windows that faced the Atlantic.

"I didn't redesign it. It was already this way. But I did buy it for its history—and the amazing views." Tulo said as he looked down at his watch. "We probably have time if you want a quick tour."

Without hesitation, Luke agreed, and for the next fifteen minutes, the men walked through the main house and guest suite. Tulo spoke with passion and eloquence as he showed off the home's clean lines and breathtaking views. The men discussed the modern design and the fine materials used to construct the home, and Luke imagined he'd like his host for the day.

Tulowitzki, or Tulo as he preferred, was a gentleman. He seemed well educated and extremely sophisticated. His well-groomed appearance and impeccable suit reminded Luke of one of his science professors at MIT. As the tour ended, Tulo made two cups of espresso, and the men were seated in the two white leather chairs overlooking the ocean. The epic windows with large glass panes made Luke feel like they were sitting outside, and he couldn't wait to hear what wisdom this man would offer.

Tulo reached into his jacket pocket and pulled out his reading glasses and a stack of white index cards. Looking up to Luke, he said, "Well, Miguel filled me in on your progress already. Just like the rest, I have some questions for you. My questions are a little different as I'm going to quiz you on a few things. I'd like you to answer as quickly as possible. If you don't know the answer, just tell me and we'll move on. These first questions will measure your aptitude, and then I will have some questions about your personal habits."

"Sounds good," Luke agreed as he leaned forward slightly, wondering what questions awaited him.

"Number one. Name the five top leaders from World War II and what country they represented. I'm looking for presidents, dictators, or prime ministers."

Luke's heart began to beat a little faster as he listened to the question about history, a subject he'd struggled with while in school. Closing his eyes to think, he tried to remember what he could. "Roosevelt was the US president. Winston Churchill was the UK prime minister. Hitler and Mussolini from Germany and Italy. Um...I'm trying, but I can't remember Japan's emperor. Sorry."

Tulo smiled. "You're doing fine, Luke. It's okay. Let's keep moving. If you remember, please tell me the capitals of these five states. New York, Michigan, Colorado, North Carolina, and Ohio."

Luke's palms began to sweat as he realized these could be very hard questions for him. "Oh man, let's see. I'm going to have to guess at a couple of these. Albany, New York. Ohio would probably be Columbus. Colorado? I think that's Denver. Lansing, Michigan, and...what was the other state?"

"North Carolina."

"Gosh, that's gotta be Charlotte? I think anyway," Luke answered, unsure of himself.

"Okay, let's keep moving. Next question. I'm going to list five inventors, and I want you to tell me what they invented. This should be easy for you though, as I read you're an MIT grad. The inventors are Alexander Gram Bell, Robert Fulton, Wilbur Wright, Johannes Gutenberg, and Karl Benz."

"Oy vey! That was a long time ago, buddy. Let's see. Bell is the telephone. Gutenberg is the printing press. Wilbur Wright was one of the Wright brothers and their plane. Benz? Known for his work in the German automotive industry. Fulton? I know it…I just can't remember off hand what he did. I'm sure it will come to me in a second."

"You're doing fine. We can come back to it. Let's move on to the next questions. Who are the four presidents on Mount Rushmore and what are they famous for? Also, can you tell me when Mount Rushmore was built and its location?"

"Hmmm…I've never been there, but I'd love to go. I'm pretty sure it's in North Dakota, but I have no idea when it was built. On it is Washington, our first president and famous for leading us in the Revolutionary War. Lincoln, who signed the Emancipation Proclamation and led the Union during the Civil War. Teddy Roosevelt is another, and he helped build the Panama Canal and established our national parks. The last guy? Oh, I don't know…Ben Franklin?"

"Sorry…Thomas Jefferson. It's okay though. The next questions are centered around your habits. In the last twelve months, how many books have you read or listened to, and what are their titles?"

Luke leaned back in his chair. "I used to read a ton, but honestly, I haven't read much this year at all. Actually, I take that back—you said listened to—and Meredith reads to me sometimes."

"What does she read to you? Can you give me the titles and authors?" Tulo asked sincerely.

Luke chuckled, knowing his host would likely take a dim view of the book. "Well, my wife reads me the Bible sometimes, but I'm not sure who to list as the author. Maybe Moses, or God?"

Whatever positive momentum Luke had when they started quickly evaporated as the questions continued. Like a bombardment, Tulo hurled question after question at Luke. What did he listen to while driving? What shows did he watch? What were the last five documentaries he watched? Who was his mentor? What are his favorite business books? What conferences did he regularly attend? Did he have a CEO peer group?

Luke could feel discouragement begin to sweep over him. Like a dark cloud, the feelings of inadequacy returned in an instant, and Luke felt extremely uncomfortable in Tulo's presence. He'd struggled with some of the other hosts' questions, but not like this. Today he felt like a complete idiot—void of any intelligence. He'd guessed on some of the first questions, trying hard to remember capitals and world history. But he utterly floundered when asked about how he spent his leisure time. Five years ago, he would have crushed it. Back then, he was an information junkie. That version of Luke was a machine fed by documentaries, business books, and leadership conferences. In his peak, Luke had mentors, coaches, and had even joined a mastermind with five other CEOs for a year.

Finally, the questions were finished, and Tulo spoke as he placed his note card and glasses back in his pocket. "Okay! That wraps up our questions and time together today. You did fine and I appreciate you answering so honestly. I'll share everything with AJ in an email tonight and you should be all set. Would you like another coffee before you go?"

Luke exhaled a huge breath without answering. After a couple more seconds, he shook his head as if he was clearing out the cobwebs. "Thank you, that would be great. My brain is feeling a little tired. I guess I should have paid more attention in middle school."

The men stood up and walked back to the kitchen when Luke suddenly comprehended Tulo's words. "Excuse me, but did you say that we're done for the day and our time is over?" The question was benign, but there was a hint of accusation in his tone.

"Yes, Luke, I have all I need—why? Was there something we missed?" Tulo responded confidently.

"Well, yes, there is! I'm not trying to complain here. You've been very kind and all, but what about the phrase? You know, the little statement about the *EntreSpirit*. Aren't you supposed to quote it to me and teach me something?" Luke said softly, feeling shortchanged by his host, who seemed to have written him off.

Tulo laughed. "Oh...you're talking about the *EntreSpirit*? You want to know about principle four. Are you sure you want to learn about that?"

"Yes! Of course! That's why I'm here, aren't I?" Luke responded, wondering why the question was so funny.

"Yes, it is," Tulo said as he finished the two coffees. He handed a cup to Luke and the men returned to their seats overlooking the ocean.

"The fourth principle is about one's pursuit of education," Tulo said after taking a sip of his drink and setting it on the table. "**The *EntreSpirit* continually EDUCATES itself. Its ferocious appetite for useful information causes it to continue learning throughout its lifetime.**"

"I see. So that's why you asked me all of those questions. You guys want to know how educated I am. That makes sense, I guess."

"Sort of, but that's not exactly correct," Tulo responded. "It isn't about your past education, but how you are pursuing your education today. That's what we're interested in."

"Well, you already know I went to MIT. I wasn't at the top of my class or anything, but I consider myself a fairly educated person. I didn't go to graduate school, but I might go back one day," Luke added, hoping his host would affirm him.

Instead, Tulo was silent, intentionally ignoring Luke's comment. Reaching for his coffee and then lifting his feet onto the ottoman, it was clear that his host was disengaged in the conversation. Luke patiently waited for nearly a minute, also sipping his coffee, but it became obvious his host wasn't going to respond.

Luke could feel himself getting annoyed, and so he decided to vocalize his frustration. "Okay, Tulo, obviously I'm missing something here and you seem to disapprove. If you've got something to say, just say it. You aren't going to hurt my feelings, so if something's on your mind, I want to hear it."

Tulo looked over at Luke and smiled. Placing his feet back on the ground, he sat up and put his coffee cup down.

"Do you really want to know?" he said, building up the suspense.

"I can take it, whatever it is. I'm tough. Go ahead! I want to know!"

"Well, I don't think you understand education. We don't care about your degree as it has nothing to do with the *EntreSpirit*. It wouldn't make the slightest bit of difference to us if you graduated from Harvard or Nova Scotia Community College. To be totally honest, your diploma is a piece of paper and doesn't tell us if you're committed to education or not."

Bothered by his host's negative comment, Luke pushed back. "Well, you can think that, but the rest of the world thinks it matters, and college was important for me. How do you think I got all of those questions right?"

"First of all, you got some of those questions wrong! Second, I didn't say that college was unimportant. I said it has nothing to do with the *EntreSpirit*. What most people do before age twenty-two is heavily influenced by their upbringing and parents. What we care about is your education as an adult—which frankly, in your case, is lacking."

Tulo sat up even taller, confident in his response, and well prepared for any debate.

"Well, without going to college, I never would have started a business. How do you explain that?" Luke asked indignantly.

"I understand that it gave you your start. It was good for you to go. I know that's how you met your business partner and how you both created CataSail. I've read about the CataSail 1000 and how it took off. Your schooling may have connected you, but what I'm saying is that it didn't fully prepare you for a life of entrepreneurship. Let's be honest here, nobody's ever prepared for that. It's like walking into a hurricane. There are thousands of moving parts and its dangers have you hanging on for dear life."

Realizing his host had studied him, Luke began to feel more unsure. Like sinking into quicksand, he slouched in his seat. His host likely knew of CataSail's downfall and was perhaps trying to prove Luke was unfit. Though tempted to cross-examine Tulo, he thought about the word he used to describe entrepreneurship—a hurricane. It was the perfect word.

If there was one thing that Luke had experience with, it was hurricanes. As a Florida native, he'd experienced many of them in his lifetime and knew their devastation.

Tulo could see Luke processing, so he continued to share. "Let me explain something that might help you. You knew a little bit about business when you graduated and opened CataSail, but not enough to be fully successful. To win and grow the company, you had to get better. It took a personal pursuit of education. How did you learn finance, leadership, hiring, operations, teamwork, or how to raise capital? Did you have a grasp on all of that when you received your diploma, or was that something you had to continue to learn as you went along?"

"I had some foundational stuff, but of course I had to keep learning as—"

"Exactly," Tulo passionately interrupted. "To win, you have to keep learning. Going to college is a good thing. For some people, it's a door into a stable career. It's also required for some professions. But it's a little different with the *EntreSpirit*. Honestly, a degree isn't one of our requirements, and some of our winners haven't even attended college. What matters to us is your ongoing education as an adult."

"With all due respect, everyone learns after college. That's a given. What I was saying is that MIT was foundational for my success, and without it, I wouldn't be where I am today."

"And where is that?" Tulo asked heatedly.

"You know what I meant!" Luke said defensively. "I meant I wouldn't have been able to build a successful business without going to MIT."

"Okay. So, what if you had a learning disability? What if you were hyperactive and struggled in school? What if you were dyslexic and had difficulty reading as a juvenile? What if your grades were so bad that MIT wouldn't accept you? What if you couldn't even get into a community college? Would you still be fit for entrepreneurship?" Tulo asked hypothetically.

"I don't know. Probably not. I went to college, so I can't say for sure, but I think that type of uneducated person probably wouldn't make it. Entrepreneurship is just too hard for most," Luke answered gruffly.

"So, Luke, you think Branson isn't fit for business then? He should hang it up because he didn't go to MIT—is that right?"

"Huh? What are you talking about, man?" Luke asked confrontationally, now sitting up tall, confused by the off-topic question.

"Sir...Richard...Branson," Tulo responded slowly, pausing between each word. "I thought you would have heard of him. You know, the billionaire business mogul who didn't graduate from high school. The guy who struggled with reading due to dyslexia? You're saying he should hang it up because he didn't go to college, right?"

"Well...no. Of course, I'm not saying that. It's just—"

Tulo interrupted as he drove his point home. "I suppose you think that everyone who doesn't have a degree is an idiot then?"

"No! I didn't say that," Luke responded defensively. "I know what you're getting at, but Richard Branson is an exception. There are exceptions to every rule and—"

Tulo interrupted again and spoke in a booming voice. "No, Luke! You are wrong! There are no rules in entrepreneurship or life. It's a hurricane and it doesn't give a crap about your diploma. No matter how prepared you think you are, you'll never be fully prepared for the storms that come. To survive, you can't count on what you learned twenty years ago! You have to get better every single day. You have to grow. You have to study and learn all the time. That's the *EntreSpirit*. It doesn't sit on its butt waiting to be spoon-fed information like a baby or count on what it learned twenty years ago. No, it pursues it like a hungry lion who is going to starve if it doesn't learn something useful every day. I'm glad you have a degree, but let's be honest, it didn't save your business, did it?"

Tulo's sharp words echoed throughout the room. This seemingly even-tempered man was now deeply passionate about the subject at hand. Like a light switch, he'd gone off on Luke, raising his voice and speaking loudly. He even had the nerve to talk about CataSail's demise. Luke was now growing tired of being interrupted and the jabs about his business folding. Looking down at his phone, he ignored his host and pretended to try to find something online, a clear sign he was ready to leave.

After a few moments of silence, Tulo cleared his throat. This time, his words were soft and sincere. "Listen, Luke. What I'm going to share with you now might surprise you, but I believe you have the *EntreSpirit*, and I'm going to recommend you without reservation. I apologize if my words seemed strong, but my goal was simply to stir you up in hopes that you'd reevaluate your approach to learning. I can tell you're a bright young man, but it seems like you're not pursuing personal growth like you used to. I hope you know that I pressed you because I see great potential in you. I like to debate, and I'm very passionate about this subject."

Luke pocketed his phone and said, "Well, I guess I have strong opinions too. I appreciate the recommendation, but I don't think it matters. I feel like I've had my butt kicked all week, and I'm not sure I have this voodoo spirit anyway."

"Don't doubt yourself. I see it—and I bet AJ and Miguel see it too. I don't know how you've done with the others, but you've done well here today. You should be proud of yourself."

Luke took a deep breath, squinting his eyes to try to understand his host's words. Looking over at Tulo, he spoke with the utmost respect. "Sir, I don't know how you could say I've done well. You said I sucked at the test and I told you I haven't done anything with my life for the last two years. To top that off, I argued with you about everything you tried to teach me. How on earth is that doing well?"

Tulo chuckled out loud. Softly at first, and then a little louder. "Luke, what you don't see is the big picture and how the contest really works. In the last couple of weeks, I've interviewed four different contestants. They were all nice and answered my questions. But each time I told them I was finished with them, they were all relieved. Only you and one other person brought up the *EntreSpirit*. For the rest, I had to bring it up myself. I had to ask them if they wanted to learn the statement. Part of one's education is asking questions. It's inquiring to know. It's the research one does to learn. Today, you kept asking when you didn't understand. You even inquired about my home, which nobody does. Everything you've done shows a tremendous curiosity and desire to learn."

"Well, I'm just a curious person, I guess," Luke said, now smiling.

"The *EntreSpirit* is a curious spirit. It loves to grow and feeds itself in many different ways. It learns from books, classes, articles, documentaries, and yes, even conversations."

As Tulo finished speaking, the doorbell rang.

13 SATISFACTION IN THE MOUNTAINS

Luke yawned as the limousine entered the sleepy little town, slowing to turn at the blinking yellow traffic light. After the two-hour flight to Asheville, he'd been in the car for over an hour. Though he didn't know what city he was in or who his last host would be, he didn't care. He was just relieved to know they'd be arriving soon. As they continued up the winding road, Luke cracked his window. The cool mountain air would help with motion sickness, but it wouldn't alleviate his anxious mind. His trip would soon be over, and the thought of the contest and how it might end began to weigh on him.

Miguel was absolutely correct when he said the trip would be a big adventure. To make it all happen, Stanton had invested a fortune, providing his private jet, fuel, accommodations, and even the million-dollar participation prize. All for what? Luke shook his head as he considered the brief meetings with each host. They were all so different and peculiar. One by one, they'd sat him down with the sole objective to teach him something about the *EntreSpirit*. They spoke with wisdom, challenging Luke to think differently about his approach to life and entrepreneurship. Though he appreciated their efforts, Luke would have preferred to spend more time with AJ and Miguel. His two guides were not only easy to talk to, but they made him feel comfortable talking about business again. Cracking the window a bit more, Luke sighed. He had expected the contest to be a quick diversion from his problems. However, as each day passed, something was changing. AJ, Miguel, and his various hosts were somehow breaking through. Never in his entire life had he been around people like this before. They spoke words that encouraged him and cut deep inside, almost in the same breath.

As the driver rounded another steep corner, a large wave of nausea crept over Luke, causing him to roll the window down all the way. It wasn't just the winding roads but the thought of losing the contest and returning to his old life. The luxury jet would no longer carry him high above his troubles. AJ and Miguel would move on without him, hosting and interviewing other contestants, but he would go home to face the ugliness that a failed company leaves behind. Afraid he might actually vomit, Luke began to spit his saliva out the window as he wiped the cold sweat from his forehead. Fortunately for Luke, he wouldn't have to endure the winding roads or his nauseous thoughts much longer. The limousine finally slowed, pulling to the side of the road. The driver quickly exited the vehicle and, coming to Luke's door, he spoke to him through the open window.

"I'm sorry, sir, but they've told me that I wouldn't be able to make it up to the house. I guess it is pretty steep and hard to turn around up there with this size vehicle. They said you could walk to the top."

Luke didn't care. He just wanted the winding hills to stop. "That's fine. Do you know how far it is?" he said as he exited the car.

"It can't be more than a half-mile or so. I can call the office to check if you'd like," the driver responded.

"No, that's all right. I can walk."

Trudging up the gravel driveway, Luke found himself pleased to be outside in the fresh cool air. A passing cold front and rain shower had left the road slightly muddy from the day before. Luke didn't know how steep the incline was, but he imagined it would take a four-wheel-drive vehicle to make it to the top. Within a few minutes, Luke was halfway up the mountain road, huffing and puffing as sweat poured from his brow.

An unfortunate event then happened. His right foot landed on some muddy clay that caused him to slip forward. Thankfully, he landed on his knee and didn't fall back down the steep incline. Standing up, a large patch of brown mud covered his blue jeans, which he tried to wipe off. This only made it worse as the spot grew larger and more noticeable with the streaks left by his muddy fingers.

By the time Luke reached the top, he was completely out of breath and stood for two full minutes before continuing. The view, however, was breathtaking. Overlooking the Smokies, a small cabin—no more than six hundred square feet—had been carefully placed on the mountainside. Complete with wraparound decking and rocking chairs, its quaintness made Luke smile as he read the large white sign attached to the wall. *Pop Pop's Cottage. If I'm Here, I'm Working.* Luke shook his head, wondering what personality he'd meet today. Continuing, he passed a rock fire pit with four chairs and a black Mercedes SUV. As he stepped onto the deck, he paused again to pull himself together before knocking on the white french doors.

Knock, knock, knock. Luke waited, but there was no answer.

Again, he pounded on the door, but this time a little louder. Knock, knock, knock. "Hello? Anyone home?"

Shielding the glare with his hands, Luke peered through the glass doors and into the cabin. Pine wall paneling with shiny lacquer covered the walls and ceiling. Though small, the unit was nicely furnished, offering a table for four, a queen-sized bed, and a full-sized sofa. A small kitchenette with a stainless-steel stove and standard size refrigerator anchored the back wall, with a sliding glass door that overlooked the back deck and view. In the opposite corner, a flat-screen TV was mounted to the wall above a small table and lamp.

Again, Luke knocked, and again, there was no answer. Pulling out his phone, the idea to call Miguel was eliminated as soon as he realized the remote location lacked cellular service. He considered heading back to the limo, but the thought of hiking the muddy hill again wasn't appealing. After all, perhaps his host was in the shower or maybe even out for a hike. Though Luke had been sweating, the cool air gave him a chill. Contemplating where he'd sit and wait, he decided to head around to the other side of the cabin, which likely offered sunshine and a better view. As he approached a small patch of sunlight near the railing of the deck, the view overlooking the Smokies enraptured him.

Standing there, Luke noticed a red figure move out of the corner of his eye. Facing away from him on a wooden picnic table, he now spotted his host, hacking away on a laptop some fifteen feet away. He couldn't see the man's face, but he could see his red jacket and bald head that moved to the silent music that played through a pair of headphones. Before Luke could approach him, the man began to move his arms violently. Acting as if he were composing a symphony orchestra, he shook and jerked his body back and forth. After the performance of a lifetime that lasted nearly twenty seconds, he slowly stopped and bowed to receive an imaginary applause. Then lifting his head again, he continued to type on his computer. Luke chuckled to himself as he waited, not wanting to embarrass the man. Once he was confident the concert was finished, he moved a couple of feet closer.

"Hello, sir," Luke said loudly, but there was no answer. Luke moved five steps closer and tried again, this time even louder.

"Sir! Hello!"

This time the man heard him, and it scared him terribly. Jumping up and throwing his headphones, the man looked at Luke as he placed his hand over his chest, confirming his heart was still there.

"You just about scared me to death!" the man exclaimed as he turned to exit the picnic table.

"I'm sorry, sir. I'm Luke Voightmann. I'm here for the contest. Is this the right place?"

"Holy crap! Is it Friday? Oh my gosh! I'm sorry. I'm so sorry. I messed up. I apologize," the man said as he closed his laptop and picked up his headphones from the ground.

"Come on in," the man said as he opened the sliding glass door on the deck. "I totally forgot what day it was. Please tell AJ I apologize when you see him again."

Continuing inside, he left Luke to close the door behind him. Frantically, the man began to straighten up the small cabin. Holding his laptop in one hand and opening a small bag with another, he stowed his computer and attached the headphones to the handle. A stack of newspapers piled high on the table was his second objective, and he quickly discarded them into a nearby wastebasket. Almost in one smooth motion, he grabbed and disposed of a half-eaten bagel and paper plate that sat on the table. Without saying a word, he moved on to the bathroom. The sound of Lysol being sprayed and a toilet flushing followed. Finally, the man returned to his guest, who he greeted with a smile.

"Again, I'm so sorry about that. Tell me your name one more time," he said as he headed for the table.

"I'm Luke Voightmann."

"Ah yes, the sailor. I got ya. We saw you on TV for a while there. Grab a seat and let's get started," the man said as he pulled out a chair across from Luke. "So I guess you know how this works by now. I've got a few questions for you. You want a glass of water or anything before we get started?"

"No thanks. I'm all set," Luke responded.

Without saying a word, the man jumped up, grabbed two glasses, and placed them on the counter. After quickly filling them with water from a pitcher in the fridge, he kicked the door shut and sat back down at the table.

"You did say you wanted some water, right?" the man said as he pushed a glass over to Luke's side of the table.

"Actually, you changed my mind. I'd love a glass. Thank you," Luke replied as he pulled the glass a little closer.

"Oh, I'm sorry about that. I'll be all right in a few minutes. I've been at it since four-thirty this morning, and sometimes I get a bit consumed. I just need a minute or two to decompress," the man said as he stood up again. "I've gotta find those note cards they sent me about you. Give me a minute to figure out where I put them."

As the man started searching, Luke chuckled at his host's quirkiness. He seemed quite scatterbrained as he frantically opened and shut drawers, hunting for the cards. A second time, he searched the same set of drawers, but he still didn't find them.

"Where the heck did I put those notes? They've gotta be here somewhere. This place ain't that big."

Luke shook his head in amusement, marveling at how quickly the man seemed to do everything. Like a hyperactive kid, he moved with energy and pop. Probably in his mid- to late-fifties, his gray hair and beard were unkempt, almost as if he hadn't bathed in days. All the hair that remained on his balding head now hung down on his right side. It covered his ear, and Luke imagined the man must use the combover approach to hide his bald head. Under his jacket, he wore a rather loose-fitting tan-colored T-shirt, which had a large spaghetti stain just below the collar. The man was a complete enigma to Luke, but at least he was entertaining.

"I got it. They're in my truck. I'll be right back!" The door flew open and several seconds later, Luke's host returned with a stack of white cards in hand. Almost gliding across the room, he sat down in such haste that it jarred the table, spilling a few drops of their water glasses. Ignoring his irreverent behavior and fixing his eyes on the note cards, he now realized he didn't have his reading glasses on, which again removed the man from the table until he found them in his laptop case. Finally, he began to read aloud what was written on the cards as he walked back to the table.

"Unsure about his work-life balance. May take his work too seriously. Highly competitive," the man said as he read the first card, sounding as though he were reading a performance review. He read the second card to himself as he sat down slowly and then looked at Luke over the brim of his glasses.

"Well, that's not good news," the man said as he shuffled the card to the back.

"What's not good news?" Luke asked.

"It says you may have neglected your health and family," the man said. "Is that true?"

Thinking about his host's erratic behavior and how deep the conversation was heading, Luke decided to take a couple of steps back. "Yes, that was true for a season. Mainly right after the accident. I was working too hard to save our company, but that isn't who I am all the time. I'm a good father and husband. But before we go any further, could you tell me your name, sir? I didn't catch it when we first met."

"I'm sorry, Luke. My name's Fred. I apologize. It's a pleasure to meet you," he said as he shook Luke's hand frantically.

Continuing to the third card, he read out loud, "Okay, here we go. Says that you're passionate and emotional, you likely possess and understand principle number five. Well, that's good news. This should be easy for us then."

"Okaaaay," Luke said, slowly trying to make sense of his host's words. "Can you tell me exactly what I have?"

"You're satisfied with your work! I've never met an *EntreSpirited* man who isn't! The statement goes like this: **The *EntreSpirit* finds great SATISFACTION in its work, often leading to seasons of imbalance. Internally driven to achieve, it enjoys its creation and watching it grow**."

Fred smiled at Luke and, removing his glasses, he said, "Does that sound like you? If so, I imagine people have called you a workaholic before."

"Well, sort of. They didn't use that word, at least not to my face, but something like that, I suppose. You have to do what it takes sometimes," Luke admitted with a grin. "What does that have to do with having the *EntreSpirit* though? I know lots of people who work hard."

"We'll get to that, but first, let me ask you some questions. I want to make sure I'm correct about a few things. Then I'll give you plenty of time to ask me anything you want. I don't think this will take too long. Would that be okay?" As he finished speaking, Fred suddenly realized his hair was out of place. Using the condensation from his glass, he began to move his hair to the top of his head.

"That's fine, sir. I'm an open book," Luke said.

"So, let's talk about the good days with CataSail. Before your partner passed away and all of the tragedy. During those earlier days, how many hours, on average, did you work each week?"

Luke shifted in his seat. "Probably fifty hours or so. Sometimes a little more. Sometimes a little less. Each week was different, I guess."

Fred nodded. "Okay, and did you ever think about work or do any work at home?"

"Of course," Luke confirmed.

"How about on vacation? Were you thinking or talking about Cata-Sail when you were away?" Fred continued the questions.

"Not all the time, but sometimes I guess I did. Even on vacation, owning a company is part of your life. What's wrong with that?" Luke asked, curious about why it mattered.

Fred didn't answer. Instead, he held up his pointer finger and continued. "Last question. Did you sometimes think a little less of others on your team who seemed to lack passion for CataSail? Think about it before you answer. I'm talking about your heart here and how you felt. How did you feel about others who didn't love CataSail or work for CataSail as hard as you did?"

Luke paused to think through his host's words, slowly cracking his knuckles as he pictured his team's faces. "Yeah...of course I thought some people on my team should've worked harder. I know every boss thinks that though. It wasn't everyone, but some of my leaders—especially Dellin at times—needed to pull more weight. I'd start complaining, and then Meredith would remind me that there was more to life than work. I don't know, sometimes I'd get annoyed, I guess."

Fred scratched his beard as he listened to Luke. "Okay, that's good. Tell me about a time when you and Dellin got into it. Think about the details and what happened. What did you say to him?"

"Well, I remember one issue. It happened maybe a year before the accident. One of our top managers left the company, and I was ticked. This guy was extremely sharp and could run multiple crews. He could build more boats than two of our other managers combined, and I was upset that Dellin couldn't handle him," Luke said, thinking about the history of his company.

"What happened? Why did your top guy leave?" Fred continued his questions.

"Because Dellin wasn't doing his job. He was supposed to be managing this guy but was taking tons of time off. Europe, Mexico, an African safari—I bet he was gone two weeks a month during that season. I told him that if he was doing a better job and working more, we wouldn't have lost the guy. The manager told me that Dellin didn't know the new designs because he was gone so much. He said that Dellin was hard on him, and he was sick of being micromanaged. I even offered him a fifty-thousand-dollar raise to stay, but he still left."

"Hmmm. That's interesting," Fred said as he took a sip of his water. "That all makes more sense now."

"What makes sense?" Luke said, unsure of how the man could truly draw any conclusions from what he just said.

"Luke, please let me try to explain something that might help you understand the *EntreSpirit*. Just hear me out for a couple of minutes and try not to interrupt. I'm going to make a few assumptions about you because I believe you have this spirit. If I'm right with these assumptions, I think it will help you. Sound good?"

"Sure. Go for it!" Luke said.

"If you have the *EntreSpirit,* then you loved to work—and were deeply satisfied by it. Your endeavor was creating CataSail, and you would rather work on CataSail than do almost anything else in the world. You see, Luke, I believe you had deep satisfaction in what you did. So much so that it wasn't enough to work forty hours. No! You had to work at home. Even on vacation, you'd work and bring CataSail with you. You could sit and work for hours and it would feel like only minutes had passed. You came in early. You stayed late. You were sad on Friday afternoon and didn't want to say goodbye because CataSail was more than just a company, CataSail was something you loved. It was like a child. You remember when it was a twinkle in your eye. It was born out of your labor. As it grew up, you babied it. You cared for it and found deep satisfaction in its health. You were proud of it, and that's why the loss of your company is so deeply painful for you."

"Like most entrepreneurs, I loved what I did, and I miss it terribly," Luke said softly.

"You know why you were always working, Luke?" Fred said to his guest.

"Why?"

"You were always working because CataSail didn't feel like work to you. It was a joy! You were deeply satisfied with your work. Does that make sense?"

"It does make sense, and it's true. I never felt like I was working, but that doesn't help me feel better. I know I loved my company. Everyone knew that! They've all moved on, though, and I'm still stuck here. Honestly, I just don't know what to do or who I am anymore," Luke said emotionally.

"Hang in there, we'll get to that. But first, you need to understand something. If you want to know why everyone else has moved on, that's simple. They didn't have the *EntreSpirit,* and CataSail wasn't their satisfaction. Even this partner of yours, Dellin. My guess is that he didn't have the *EntreSpirit* either."

Luke looked up in surprise and objected, "Now hold on a second. How can you say he didn't have the *EntreSpirit*? You've never even met him!"

Fred now spoke more carefully to honor the deceased, "I'm sorry if that bothers you, Luke. Don't misunderstand me. I'm sure Dellin was a good man, just not someone with the *EntreSpirit*. Honestly, whose idea was it to start the company?"

"Both of ours, I guess. Maybe I drove it a little harder, but we both agreed," Luke said.

Fred pushed back. "Okay, but would he have started CataSail without you? Let's say you backed out at the last minute. What would have happened then?"

Luke paused for a moment to consider Fred's question and then spoke softly as he thought through his friend's life. "Dellin was never sure about CataSail. Raising the money, moving to Miami, naming the company—all of that was me. After his father died, he thought about selling his shares and retiring. I wouldn't let him."

"Don't feel bad, Luke. CataSail just wasn't his satisfaction. He was a co-founder and your partner. He did great work and served you as a very good executive, but he didn't live and breathe CataSail. You wanted him to love it as you did, but how could he? His satisfaction was found in something else. What you don't understand is that even though he was a great friend and business partner, it would be impossible for him to love CataSail as you did. It isn't wrong, and it doesn't make him less of a man either. It just explains why you two were different. Does that help any?"

"I don't know. I've never thought about it like that before," Luke answered, now staring at the table.

"Here is another thought that will rattle your brain. Your manager that performed so well—that guy probably had the *EntreSpirit*. It sounds like he was driven and passionate about building boats. He found satisfaction in his work and wanted to create more but struggled because he felt micromanaged. Whatever happened to him?" Fred asked, not knowing how impactful his question would be.

"That's unbelievable you would ask that question. Unbelievable!" Luke said shaking his head. "About the time we were closing, I found out that guy was opening a shipyard to build catamarans. Two months ago, I heard he was slammed and had picked up a lot of our contracts. He even raised a bunch of money to expand."

"Ah, yes, just as I thought. That's the *EntreSpirit*."

For the next forty minutes, Luke asked question after question. Fred, who once seemed discombobulated, became razor-focused and a wealth of information as he explained the beauty of truly loving one's work. He shared how *EntreSpirited* leaders have the best life because they never feel like they're working. He compared their stories to the trapped executives who hate their jobs and the unhealthy companies that employ them. As Fred continued, Luke's heart became encouraged as he now understood why he felt so different about business and CataSail.

"Luke, I've truly enjoyed our time together. Unfortunately, I've gotta be getting back to work here pretty soon. Do you have any other questions for me before I let you go?"

Luke didn't really want to leave, but he didn't have any more questions either. Shaking his head, he said, "No, sir. I don't think so. I appreciate what you've shared. Now I just need to figure out what I'm going to do with the rest of my life."

As the words left Luke's mouth, reality hit him that he had no idea what he was going to do. There were major battles ahead and the thought of starting over began to burden him. Slowly, Luke's head sank low as he looked at his folded hands on the table.

Fred couldn't help but notice the weight Luke carried and decided to encourage him, saying, "Well, I can hang out a few more minutes. Let me share a story with you. It might do you some good. Do you know why I'm up here in this cabin today?"

"Well, the sign outside says, 'If I'm Here, I'm Working,'" Luke said and both men laughed.

"Right! I come up here to do my work. What you don't know is my full name is Fredrick J. LeMahieu. Does that ring a bell?" the man said.

"The writer? No way! I've heard of you. My wife has read one of your books. She told me about it one night while we were sitting in bed—something about a guy who hunts down women who were caught cheating on their husbands. That's you?" Luke said in shock with wide-open eyes.

"Yes. That's me!" he said, smiling. "My friends call me Fred though. I come here to write my stories. It's what I do, and it brings me great satisfaction. I can write all day, and it doesn't feel like work. But I didn't start out writing novels. Out of college, I got a job for the local paper as a crime reporter. That was my primary responsibility, but I also had a few other topics I covered. I loved my work. For me, it was the most exciting thing I'd ever done. I wasn't married at the time, and so I wrapped myself up in my work. I'd listen to the police scanner and then drive around taking pictures, interviewing deputies, and learning about all sorts of crazy mysteries. I was kind of famous for a season and even gave testimony in court to help convict a murderer. My boss loved my work, and I was content with staying."

"Sounds like an interesting job," Luke said, wondering if that was how he came up with the ideas for his novels.

"It was indeed. Then I got married. She seemed like a nice gal at first, but I later realized she had major insecurities and emotional problems. We'd only known each other for three months when she faked a pregnancy to rope me into a marriage. If she was willing to do that, imagine what our marriage was like! I wanted to continue to write for the paper, but my new wife demanded that I give up reporting and get a job that paid better. Wanting to be a good husband, I reluctantly did what she asked. We relocated to Staten Island, where I took a job as the editor for a book publisher in the city. It paid big bucks, but I was miserable because I wasn't writing, and I had an hour-long commute to work every day. I stayed there for three very long years and hated every minute of it."

"So, how did you get back to writing?" Luke asked.

"My wife met some guy at the park and started cheating on me. One night I came home to an empty house and a note that said she wanted a divorce. She cleaned out our bank accounts and took every single item out of the house, even my boxer shorts and socks, just to be spiteful."

Luke couldn't help but snicker as he pictured the woman removing his host's underwear.

"Wow! Even your clothes? That's cold-hearted! What did you do?"

"Though my wife was crazy, I loved her and was devastated. I moved back home with my parents. For a long time, I floundered, feeling sorry for myself. I remember delivering pizzas at night, and then I'd come home and cry myself to sleep. I felt so empty. I tried to get a job reporting again, but my old boss had left, and the paper wasn't hiring. I felt so defeated and broken, and that's when it hit me. I loved to write, and I didn't need a job to start writing again! It became my entrepreneurial outlet and where I found deep satisfaction. Because I was in the publishing business, I knew what would sell. The story came easy to me too because of what my ex-wife had done. I admit, the book was a little twisted, but so was I back then. It took me three months to finish, but I wrote my novel and connected with a young literary agent I'd worked with a couple of years before. I guess you could say the rest is history. The book was published, and it went on to be a best seller. I married my literary agent two years later, and now we have four kids and two granddaughters who call me Pop Pop. I'm rich now too, so everything worked out great!"

Luke smiled as he listened to the poetic justice of the story, wondering if Fred's ex-wife had ever read the novel.

"Let me encourage you with this, Luke. Don't give up. Many entrepreneurs believe their business satisfied them, but that's just not true. CataSail didn't bring you satisfaction—it wasn't the company, but how you enjoyed building it and working on it. If you truly have the *EntreSpirit*, I'm sure you'll build something else and will love every minute of that too."

"Thank you, sir. I appreciate your encouragement and many kind words. I know I'll be okay one day. I guess it's just hard sometimes to think about rebuilding because I didn't just lose my company. I lost my best friend too."

Fred smiled brightly. Seeming to see something that Luke couldn't, he continued in a gentle tone. "Ah, but have you ever sat down to think about where Dellin found his satisfaction?"

"Not really. I just know it wasn't CataSail," Luke said.

Fred continued, "I imagine he found great satisfaction in his adventures. That explains why he took so many vacations and why he wanted to deliver the boat to the senator."

"Yeah, he definitely lived for adventure," Luke added, wondering where his host might be going.

"I think there's something else that you might not have seen," Fred said, and then carefully paused out of respect. "Though CataSail wasn't Dellin's satisfaction, I believe he did love being there. I never had the privilege of meeting him, but I'd be willing to bet that he took great pleasure in being your friend, partner, and supporting you as you grew the company. My guess is that he never wanted the spotlight and was happy to just help you. I also believe that he stayed at CataSail because he wanted to. He was a grown man after all, and if he wanted to sell his shares, he could have done so. He stayed because he loved the adventure and being with you. Be encouraged, Luke. You shouldn't feel bad about Dellin's death. More than anything, you should try to realize how much he must have cared about you."

As Luke listened to Fred speak tenderly about Dellin, he froze, unable to move or respond. Instead, he stared down at the table, picturing his best friend's face. Realizing the depth of Dellin's love and friendship, Luke's eyes softened until two large drops slowly rolled down his cheeks. For eighteen months, Luke had carried this heavy burden, blaming himself for his friend's death. But Fred put things in a different light. Indeed, Dellin could have sold his shares if he really wanted to. He also didn't have to deliver the boat to the senator. He did it because it was an adventure, and he died doing what he loved. Even his faithfulness to CataSail showed his love for Luke. Like an arrow to the heart, Fred had somehow changed Luke's paradigm. He showed him something that was there all along, and hearing it, Luke's bottled-up tears poured out.

14 LESSONS ALONG THE WAY

"You okay? You've barely spoken a word," AJ said sincerely as the plane lifted off from Asheville. With Miguel working on something in the galley, Luke sat across from AJ in the rear cabin. At last, he had reached the final leg of his trip. Knowing he'd be meeting Stanton soon and learn the fate of the contest, Luke's mind was elsewhere as he stared down at the floor.

"I'm okay, sir. Thank you. I guess I have a lot on my mind."

"I'm sure you do. You've been busy over the last couple of days. You met with Tulo and Fred, right?" AJ said.

He didn't wait for Luke's response to continue. "Tulo is probably one of the most difficult hosts because of all the quizzing he does. People tell us that he's extremely hard to read because you never know where you stand with him. That tends to cause some stress on contestants. Be encouraged though—he told us that you did very well. Also, I hear you had a good time with Fred. He's one of the favorites and one of my very dear friends."

Luke scratched his head as he thought of his last two hosts. "Yeah, Tulo threw me off a bit. The other hosts have shared the principles right away, but he made me dig for it. It ended up being fine, and he taught me something about myself. And Fred—how could anyone not like him? What a funny guy! For a minute, I felt like I was in a therapy session. He had a lot of great insights and helped me make sense of some things I've struggled with for a while. I do have a question or two, if that's okay."

"Absolutely. That's why I'm here," AJ confirmed.

Luke leaned forward a little and said, "Well, I've been thinking about this. You've tried to get me to understand each host and why they have this *EntreSpirit* thing. But what about my last two hosts? I don't even know what Tulo does. And how do you consider Fred to be an entrepreneur? Don't get me wrong, I really liked him, and he is a creative guy. I just don't see how being a writer connects to the *EntreSpirit*." Having completed his thoughts, he leaned back in his chair, waiting to hear AJ's response.

"Let's start with Tulowitzki," AJ answered. "You might have guessed that's a Polish name. To understand what he taught you about the principle of education, you probably need to understand his story. His daddy's family migrated from Poland after World War II. I know they suffered terribly during that time and all of them were in a concentration camp. When they came over, it was in the late forties and his daddy was a young teenager, maybe thirteen or fourteen. Anyway, the family moved to a small Polish village, and that's where his momma and daddy met. I'm missing some details, but I know they ended up getting married and buying a small wheat farm in Ontario, and that's when Tulo came along. He's the oldest of seven children. Because his mother and father didn't speak English, they insisted the children go to school. By the way, did he tell you about the history of his house?"

"Yeah, he said it was some sort of gunning tower, but I didn't know his parents were in a concentration camp!" Luke said in surprise.

"Well, now you know why he had to buy it when it came on the market. Anyway, Tulo's family needed help on the farm. There were a lot of mouths to feed, so he didn't end up going to high school. Instead, he spent his days tending to his chores. They didn't have much money, but the town did have a library. Every weekend he'd check out all kinds of books and that's how he's learned so much. He often jokes that he read self-help books before it was cool to read them. He's never been through formal schooling, but you'd never know it. He's one of the brightest guys you'll ever meet. He reads dozens of books each year and is always studying something."

"That explains why he wasn't too impressed with my degree," Luke added, remembering their conversation.

AJ nodded. "Well, I know he's thought about going to college. He told me one time that he inquired about it, but there were a bunch of hoops to jump through because he didn't go to high school. Anyway, as he got older, he became interested in business, but not by choice. When he was about eighteen, his father passed away, and Tulo took over the farm. One day, he had an idea to rent and develop the neighboring land in exchange for a percentage of profits. It's a long story, but he took the profits and bought more land to farm on. When he eventually sold the farms, he started learning about real estate. He kept learning and built a multimillion-dollar real estate company. He's pretty much retired now, but he still does a little consulting and sits on several boards."

"I guess that's why he's passionate about education, but not necessarily in the traditional context."

"Well, not just him. All of us," AJ said. "Entrepreneurship is evolving. The challenges for entrepreneurs are greater today than ever before. It's a global economy and your competition isn't just the guy down the street. To win, companies need to understand social media, politics, pandemics, legislation, and all sorts of challenges I never had to face when I was a young man. That's why we look for people who love to learn." Again, from memory, AJ spoke the principle. "**The *EntreSpirit* continually EDUCATES itself. Its ferocious appetite for useful information causes it to continue learning throughout its lifetime.**"

The statement, Tulo's story, and AJ's words now made sense to Luke, who said, "I used to learn everything I could about business. I've gotta get back to reading when I get home."

AJ smiled. "One thing I'd encourage you with, young man, is that you shouldn't just focus on reading. Focus on growing. Watch a documentary or have a conversation with somebody who knows more than you. Go to a seminar. Listen to an audiobook or podcast. Everyone learns in different ways. Figure out how to build it into your schedule and make it a habit to get a little better every day. Learning should be part of your life, never a chore."

"I used to do that, sir, and I'm going to get back to it."

"You want me to tell you about Fred now?" AJ asked sincerely. "You had some questions about him, didn't you?"

"Yes, the writer!" Luke said. "What's funny is my wife has read one of his books. I'm just curious about how you believe that ties in with business."

"Well, let me explain something to you first. If you look up the definition of an entrepreneur, you'll usually find some description of someone willing to risk a loss to make money. Others call it the pursuit of opportunity that others don't see. There are a lot of definitions, but most of them make entrepreneurship sound like you're chasing a carrot at the end of a stick. However, in my mind, it is clear. When you look up the root words, it simply means 'one who undertakes in enterprise,'" AJ said as he wiped his lips.

Standing up, he took a few steps forward to the fridge built into the credenza and grabbed two cans of Diet Coke. Returning, he handed one to Luke and then sat down. After popping the can open, he took a sip and then continued.

"Fred doesn't have employees. There's no chairman of the board, shareholders, or executives. It's just him. To some, that might not be an enterprise, but how I define it, it is."

Luke nodded. "It's different, but he shared his story with me. He took some risks and seems to be doing pretty well. Nobody can argue with that, I guess."

"Right!" AJ said. "And here's why I call that entrepreneurship. Actually, you can help me with this. Take a minute and think about why people become entrepreneurs. In other words, why do people start businesses? Why did you start CataSail?"

Luke opened his soda can as he thought. "One reason is probably money. They want to be financially secure and have nice things."

"Check!" AJ said, nodding his head.

"Flexibility," Luke said next. "They want to control their schedule and don't want someone telling them when they need to clock in."

"Check!" AJ agreed for the second time.

"Free time might be another one. They want to work less, spend more time with their family, go on vacations, enjoy the holidays, and things like that."

"Check again!" AJ responded. "Keep going, young man!"

"I'd say influence is another. Running a business gives you a certain amount of influence and prestige."

"Check! You're spot on with that one! Anything else you can think of, Luke?" AJ asked.

"There are other smaller things, but I'd say that is probably the top four reasons why people might start a business. It's a dream come true for a lot of people."

AJ smiled and said, "You did good, but you missed one big reason, which I'll explain in a minute. Now, let's consider Fred and the questions you just asked. Does Fred make a lot of money from writing?"

"I see where you're going with this. Yes, he makes great money and has a lot of flexibility and free time," Luke responded.

"And a ton of influence too! He makes millions every year. He has the flexibility to go anywhere at any time. He has unlimited free time and takes six weeks off every summer to travel with his family. Wouldn't you say that he has everything people want when they start a business?"

"No question. He's got it all. Actually, it sounds like a great business model if you ask me!"

AJ let out a hearty laugh, which made Luke feel good. "I've been telling him that for years! He's got the best business in the world," AJ said as he pressed the recline button on the sofa to prop his feet up. "But where was he this morning?"

"His cottage?" Luke said, not fully understanding the question.

"No, I meant what was he doing at the cottage? Did you read the sign out front?" AJ asked, hoping Luke would see the truth.

Luke's eye's widened as the light bulb went off. "He was working. Pop Pop's cottage. If I'm here, I'm working," Luke said, quoting the sign that hung on the wall. "Let me guess what I missed. People become entrepreneurs because they love what they do. Is that right?"

"Check! You got it!" AJ said excitedly to his pupil, now deeply pleased with Luke's desire to learn. Continuing, AJ spoke the statement that was connected to the last principle. "**The *EntreSpirit* finds great SATISFACTION in its work, often leading to seasons of imbalance. Internally driven to achieve, it enjoys its creation and watching it grow.**"

"That statement describes me to the T!" Luke said as he chuckled.

"Me too!" AJ added as he joined Luke in a laugh. "It's hard for me to imagine, but so many people hate their jobs. Every day they hate getting out of bed because their work isn't fulfilling. They continue to stay because of a paycheck, but never really enjoy what they do. You've done very well this week. I'm proud of you and all of your progress."

Feeling encouraged, Luke pressed the recline button and lifted his feet. Taking another sip of soda, he thought of his two guides, AJ and Miguel. The two men seemed so content in their roles and Luke imagined they must love their jobs. After thinking for a moment, he decided to ask a difficult but important question.

"AJ, could I ask you something else? It's kind of personal and it's okay if you don't want to answer it," Luke said, slightly lowering his seat so he could see AJ better.

"Sure. I'm happy to help if I can," AJ affirmed.

"Well, I'm not sure how to ask this—it's just that you and Miguel are probably the two happiest employees I've ever met. You know all about the *EntreSpirit* and entrepreneurship. However, you both seem so comfortable in your roles. Isn't it hard not to be an entrepreneur? Don't get me wrong, you guys are amazing. I guess what I'm asking is, don't you struggle with this? I just don't know if I could ever be an employee again. I don't know if that makes any sense. I'm just curious if it is hard for you guys?"

AJ didn't move a muscle. He sat for a full five seconds with a smile across his face. Had he not been smiling, Luke might have assumed he offended the man. Finally, AJ said, "Luke, there's something I don't think you're seeing here. I am an entrepreneur. Just because someone works as an employee doesn't mean they don't have the *EntreSpirit*. Every single leader at Stanton Enterprises is an entrepreneur. It's a requirement for getting hired here. We are all owners of our departments, trusted to manage and guide them, just as if they were our own companies."

"But what about the benefits of entrepreneurship? What about the money, flexibility, freedom, and all of that stuff? Don't you miss all of that?" Luke curiously asked.

"I see. Now I understand what you're after," AJ said as he pressed a button to bring the couch upright. "Let me see if I can rephrase what you're looking for. You want to know why anyone would be willing to give up the money, flexibility, freedom, and prestige, or all the perks of entrepreneurship, to take a W-2 job—is that right?"

"Yes! I can't imagine anyone trading all of that in," Luke added passionately.

AJ smiled brightly, extremely pleased with Luke's question. "You've just hit the nail on the head, young man. Understanding this principle is the secret sauce of having the *EntreSpirit* thrive in any organization."

"What principle?" Luke asked trying to make sense of AJ's words.

"The principle that you have to treat *EntreSpirited* leaders like partners and fellow entrepreneurs. You see, the *EntreSpirit* hates being cooped up. It's just not in their DNA. They want to achieve and create and if they can't do that in their role, they'll never be content to stay. The *EntreSpirit* is a 'get it done spirit,' and if you hire *EntreSpirited* people, they're going to move the needle. The leader's job sometimes is to get out of their way. There's a lot to leading the *EntreSpirit*, but I'll tell you what matters most is trusting them and empowering them to lead. You simply can't micromanage the *EntreSpirit*. Right behind that is giving them total flexibility with their schedule. Equally important is excellent compensation. They ought to be paid so well that they never want to leave. Lastly, all of that has to be built into the organization, starting with the CEO and passed down to every department leader." AJ understood the principle deeply and spoke passionately as if he'd learned the lesson from firsthand experience.

Fully engaged in the conversation, Luke added a few of his own thoughts. "That makes sense. I've never really considered hiring entrepreneurs. I just know how I am and I imagine it would be extremely difficult to employ someone like myself who has had all the benefits of entrepreneurship."

"Difficult? Yes! Impossible? Not hardly. Though it might not be easy, the payoff is huge. You see, when you hire leaders with the *EntreSpirit*, they don't just add value, they multiply it. They are leaders of leaders! They lighten the load and instantly make a big impact. They break up the leadership bottleneck, and instead of having one person driving growth, there's a whole team of people. Imagine if you could have cloned yourself to help CataSail. Wouldn't that have made a huge difference?" AJ asked, trying to get Luke to connect the dots.

"Sure, it would have helped us. I'm just not sure that was possible in our situation," Luke answered, missing the point.

AJ snapped back. "But it is possible! If you didn't do it, it's simply because you were afraid to rock the boat—no pun intended. If you understood the principles, you could have made changes to your team. You could have hired the *EntreSpirit* and partnered with them to lead your organization. Instead of carrying everything yourself, you could have led high caliber, *EntreSpirited* leaders! That's what I call cloning yourself!"

Luke waited to respond. He sat there thinking about AJ's words as they slowly began to sink in. In slow motion, his trip, lessons, and hosts' words all began to come together, and he realized something he hadn't seen before. The *EntreSpirit* wasn't about owning a business, but the heart of an individual. It lived in nonprofits, hospitals, schools, and governments. It was everywhere and in all types of people, regardless of their ethnicity, age, or gender. From the mission field in Peru to a cottage in North Carolina, he had seen it in action, and it began to click.

Looking up at AJ, he asked, "Miguel has the *EntreSpirit* too, right?"

AJ nodded in agreement. "He's passionate about the company's mission. He loves entrepreneurs and helping them do great things. He's a big part of the contests and has helped many contestants overcome and get back on their feet. His vision is clear, and he gets to think about all sorts of ideas. We used to fly our hosts in for the contests, but getting them to all take a week at the same time was nearly impossible. The trips were Miguel's idea. He did that to make us better. He's always growing and learning from everyone he meets. He has plenty of time to read, study, and learn when he's not working. Does he love his job? I think so! He takes eight weeks of vacation every year and is compensated very well with plenty of bonuses. And look at this plane—it isn't like he's suffering. Who wouldn't want to fly all over the world on this luxurious jet and stay at first-class accommodations?"

Luke laughed. "Yeah, I can see how you both would love your jobs. If I lose the contest, maybe Miguel could train me to fill in when he's on vacation. I already know all the hosts!" he said as he admired the private jet.

"So, before we land and say our goodbyes, I'll give you an easy way to remember what you've learned. All you have to do is remember the word MOVES. M-O-V-E-S. M stands for the Mission. O stands for Overcoming. V stands for Vision. E stands for Education, and S is for Satisfaction. MOVES, the *EntreSpirit* MOVES. Make sense?"

Luke smiled and said, "I love acrostics. It makes everything easier to remember. I think I've got it. Mission, overcoming, vision, education, and satisfaction—the *EntreSpirit* MOVES. Now I have the acrostic to go with my memorable experiences. I don't think I'll forget it."

"Good!" AJ responded.

Luke looked outside the window as they started their descent into Dallas. Checking his watch, he saw it was a little past six o'clock. Knowing his time with his guide was coming to an end, he wanted to express his deep gratitude to AJ for his kindness and words of wisdom. He also hoped that AJ might provide some helpful tips for meeting Stanton.

"Sir, I want to thank you for your hospitality this week. Both you and Miguel have been great. I've really enjoyed our time together and our talks. You've given me a lot to think about and a different perspective. Before we land, I was wondering if you have any tips for my weekend. I'm not nervous, but if you have any feedback for me, I'd love to hear it." Luke's words were humble as he spoke in the most respectful tone to honor AJ.

AJ smiled at Luke and said, "It's been our pleasure, young man. You've been a great contestant and have a desire to learn that's impressed all of us. I think you'll do well this weekend, and I hope you win. In regard to feedback, I'd just encourage you to have a good time and be yourself. Be the same person you've been with us this week, and I think it will turn out all right for you in the end."

15 THE INFAMOUS MR. STANTON

For the second time this week, Luke landed at the executive airport just outside of Dallas. As he followed AJ out of the airplane, the warm air engulfed him as the city's skyline came into perspective. A black stretch limo, crafted from a luxury SUV and marked with the words Stanton Enterprises, awaited the passengers. The two pilots finished transferring the luggage into the limo and said their goodbyes. Luke also thanked them for their service and then joined AJ and Miguel inside the vehicle.

Before the men could drive off, Luke spotted a white hanger about thirty feet away. The door was wide open, which allowed him to see the maintenance crew working on the plane inside. To his surprise, an identical Gulfstream 650ER was found, also bearing the words "Stanton Enterprises" along its side.

"Stanton owns two private jets?" Luke asked hastily, hardly believing that someone could need two planes.

"Yes, Mr. Luke. That is how we were able to meet you so fast this week and be with you. We use two planes because we have two contestants this week. They started last Friday and went home today though," Miguel answered, not thinking it to be a big deal.

"Could you call ahead and let them know we're on our way?" AJ asked Miguel, who nodded and picked up his mobile phone.

"We're only about fifteen minutes out, and I want to make sure they're ready for us," AJ said to Luke, who still stared into the hanger. "Having two jets allows us to host two contestants during the same week but keep them separated. But the planes are used for more than contests. We allow our CEOs to use them for business as well. Kind of a perk for being part of the Stanton family, I suppose."

As AJ finished speaking, Miguel's phone call was answered. Whoever was on the other end seemed to know him pretty well. Because the call was in Spanish, Luke didn't know what was being said, but he assumed they were making arrangements for the drop-off. Unable to speak with AJ over the call, Luke thought about the contest and his upcoming meeting. The second plane explained how AJ and Miguel could pop in and out and seem to show up at various locations, but that wasn't what concerned him. Realizing the amount of time, money, and effort that was spent on bringing him into the contest was alarming, and he wondered if he would measure up to Stanton's requirements. He probably would have continued to worry about this, but fortunately, Miguel's phone call ended.

Now sharing with everyone, Miguel said, "Everything is set for you, Mr. Luke. We will drop you off in a few minutes. They told me that you have time to take a shower and to get ready for dinner. They have a big meal for you tonight. And Mr. Stanton...he is very excited to meet you. He says he wants to ask you questions about your boat company and why it lost so much money. He said if you're not a good CEO, maybe you can work for him as his boat captain." As Miguel finished, he and AJ let out a few chuckles, informing Luke that they were messing with him.

"Oh great!" Luke said, playing along. "I can't wait to tell him about CataSail's failures. But I'd be his captain—as long as I get to use the private planes."

Now all the men laughed.

AJ bumped Luke with his elbow and said, "Whatever you do, don't let him bully you. Be tough, young man! He puts his pants on one leg at a time, just like everyone else!" AJ and Miguel continued to giggle. Seeming to know Stanton fairly well, they decided to taunt Luke about his upcoming meeting.

Miguel was enjoying himself and added, "I remember when I met him. He said, 'I can't understand a word you are saying! Are you even speaking in English?'"

"And don't let that big mansion of his scare you. Remember, everything is bigger in Texas, including people's egos. And if you happen to meet his wife, tell her that you prefer the country look of the dark wood," AJ added as he chuckled. It was now clear to Luke that they knew Stanton and his home intimately, and their jokes helped ease Luke's nerves.

"You guys aren't going to scare me. I'm ready for it," Luke said confidently, trying to reassure himself. "And if I don't end up winning this contest, Stanton's the real loser here because he doesn't know what he's missing out on!"

The men all laughed. For the remainder of the ride, they spoke about Luke's week and their adventures together. Though Luke laughed outwardly, inwardly, he was feeling a little sad. He knew he'd soon have to say goodbye to these men. In just a few days, he felt closer to them than many of his other friends. They were authentic, smart, inspiring, and fun to be around. They didn't have a hint of pretentiousness and didn't judge him for his scars and wounds. Instead, they accepted him for who he was and encouraged him to become better.

As they approached Stanton's house, Luke couldn't help but feel excited and nervous. The wrought iron gate opened, and the men continued down the long driveway. Though Luke was curious about their destination, he wanted to invest his final minutes fully focused on his two guides. They had impacted his life and somehow made it a little better. Pulling up beside the house, Luke searched for the words to express his gratitude. "I guess this is it. I don't know what to say, fellas, except thank you. Sincerely, thank you for your kindness, generosity, warmth, and the life lessons you've shared with me. Seriously, you have no idea how much you've helped me this week, and I'll be forever grateful for both of you. Regardless of what happens, I hope we can remain friends for a long time."

Luke's words might have sounded too soft, but he didn't care. It was his last chance to express himself, and he wouldn't let his pride get in the way. After the car rolled to a stop, the driver opened the door and removed Luke's bags. Luke stepped out, followed by AJ and Miguel, who wanted to give a proper goodbye. AJ shook Luke's hand firmly and offered words of encouragement. He then stepped back into the vehicle. Miguel also shook Luke's hand but then offered a hug. Luke didn't mind. They'd spent a lot of time together, and he figured it was part of Miguel's culture. Miguel then returned to the limo and Luke headed for the door.

Fixing his eyes on the grand home, he realized it was indeed spectacular. Actually, it was everything Luke expected of a billionaire. A true southerner's estate, held together with six large columns connecting the two stories. Eight white rocking chairs were spread across the entire front porch, which was probably seventy feet wide. The home's glossy white paint and striking green shutters reminded Luke of the deep south plantation homes he'd seen in movies. Looking out across the lawn, luscious gardens and flowers highlighted the estate. As he walked to the front door, he turned one last time to wave to the men as they drove away. Taking a deep breath to compose himself, he pressed the doorbell, stepped back a couple of feet, and exhaled as he waited for an answer.

Slowly, the door crept open, and a short woman appeared. Dressed in a traditional maid's outfit, she greeted Luke and said, "Hello. You must be Luke. We've been expecting you. Please come in."

Luke greeted the woman and then followed her inside to the open landing as she continued speaking. "I'll take you to your room now, sir. We'll have dinner ready in forty-five minutes. In the meantime, you can clean up and get comfortable."

The woman then grabbed Luke's rolling suitcase and proceeded to walk very quickly through the home, almost at a running pace. Luke would have liked to take in the mansion but was forced to jog just to keep up. Finally, they reached one of the guest bedrooms. The woman quickly opened the door and went inside, lifting Luke's bag onto the suitcase rack.

"I'll come to get you in forty-five minutes, sir. Okay?" she said as she exited the room.

"Yes, ma'am. I'll be ready," Luke responded as the woman closed the door.

Inspecting the bedroom, Luke noticed the large brown walls that AJ had mentioned. The wood was beautiful. Its polish made Luke imagine it to be fine mahogany, but he could certainly understand why a fresh coat of paint might be best. Though its quality was superb, the home seemed a little dated, almost as if it was created to look old. Without thinking about much else, Luke headed for the ensuite bathroom, and that's where panic struck him.

"What am I going to wear for dinner?" Luke said out loud as he turned on the shower. For the entire week, Miguel had provided his outfit, and now he was gone. Still wearing his muddy blue jeans, Luke tried to think through what he might have in his bag appropriate for meeting Stanton. Before getting into the shower, he decided to look, knowing he wouldn't be able to relax until he figured it out. As he opened his suitcase, he began to laugh out loud. Miguel had delivered once again. Tonight, he'd be well dressed. Wrapped in plastic, a red dress shirt with a bolo tie and a pair of blue jeans greeted him. Underneath, he found a brown leather belt with a large golden belt buckle. A small note was also included, which read: *AJ and I picked this outfit especially for you, Mr. Luke. Have fun tonight. Your friend, Miguel.*

Two years ago, a practical joke like this would have made Luke upset. Not anymore. Today he could do nothing but laugh at his guides' antics. They were sending him to meet Stanton dressed like a country hick. For all he knew, Stanton was probably in on the joke too. Luke shook his head as he walked into the bathroom. Within thirty minutes, he emerged, clean and freshly shaven, and dressed in the provided clothes. Again, his outfit was a perfect fit. With a few minutes to spare, Luke sat down in the easy chair in the corner of his room. Closing his eyes, he thought he might rest until the maid returned.

"Are you ready for dinner, sir?" the woman's voice said from outside the room.

"Yes, I'll be right out," Luke responded as he jumped to his feet. He didn't know if he had drifted off, but it felt like as soon as he shut his eyes, she was at the door.

From outside Luke's room, she continued speaking, "Mr. Stanton is waiting for you at the table, sir."

As Luke opened the door, the woman said, "Unfortunately, we are very late for dinner. We must move quickly now. Follow me, sir."

Late? How could they be late? he wondered to himself.

It didn't matter because he had to keep up with the woman who now dashed down the hall and back through the foyer. As they approached the large kitchen, she finally stopped and lifted her hand for him to wait. Slowly opening the dining room door, she peeked in and nodded. Backing out, she shut the door behind her, turned to Luke, and said, "Mr. Stanton is ready for you, sir. Please wait ten seconds, and then go in."

As Luke counted backward from ten, he thought that this might be the strangest dinner invitation he'd ever experienced. When his count reached zero, he opened the door. To his surprise, he saw Miguel sitting at the table with a huge smile across his face, which caused Luke to freeze in confusion. Miguel waved for Luke to come closer as he continued to grin. Next to Miguel, a man with a large cowboy hat sat at the head of the table. His head was bowed low so that Luke couldn't see his face.

As Luke approached, Miguel stood up and said, "Mr. Luke, please meet the CEO of Stanton Enterprises, Mr. Allen Jeffrey Stanton."

Tipping his hat and standing, another familiar face greeted Luke with a smile. Luke gasped out loud, almost as if he'd seen a ghost.

"Put her there, young man," he said as he reached for Luke's hand. "It's a pleasure to meet you. I'm Allen Jeffrey Stanton, but you can call me AJ. That's what my friends call me anyway."

"You're Stanton? I don't understand!" Luke exclaimed as he shook AJ's hand, still in shock.

"You should see your face, Luke! You should see it!" Miguel cried out as he started to laugh. Now laughter erupted throughout the house. From Miguel and AJ to the maids and cooks, everyone was now laughing at Luke, who was still in shock about what was happening.

"I simply don't know what to say. I feel like a complete jackass!" Luke said sheepishly, still trying to understand it all.

AJ grabbed Luke's shoulder and reassured him, "It's all good, my boy. When I realized on the plane you didn't know who I was, we all decided to have a little fun with you. That's all. We didn't expect it to go on for so long. You never asked me my last name, or we would have told you. Even when you got here and came to dinner, you walked right past a giant portrait of our family and I thought for sure you'd figure things out."

"I was wondering why she was running through the house so quickly! I'm so confused right now," Luke said in bewilderment. "I mean—how can you be Stanton? I looked you guys up online. The CEO was some guy in his forties named Michael. What am I missing?"

"Oh...you're talking about my son, Michael Stanton. He runs Stanton Yachts and is the CEO of that company. You must have seen a picture of him."

Luke finally began to understand his source of confusion. Going back in his mind, he remembered how he researched Stanton Yachts online and saw a picture of the young CEO. When AJ boarded the plane, he knew it couldn't be him and assumed he was someone that ran the contests. He had figured that the CEO of Stanton Yachts and the CEO of Stanton Enterprises was the same person—instead, they were father and son. The informal and casually dressed cowboy he met last Sunday wasn't a recruiter. No, it was the billionaire mogul himself who boarded the plane to personally meet his contestants. A whirlwind of thoughts and emotions crossed his mind as he continued to shake his head.

AJ could see Luke's mind wrestling and decided to encourage him, saying, "Don't you worry, Luke. You did great this week! Don't you dare be down on yourself for one minute! We're all really impressed with you. We even liked the fact that you didn't know who I was because it allowed you to be more authentic. We're talking about building that into our contest moving forward, all because of you."

As the men sat down and drinks were poured, Luke tried to wrap his head around everything. Slowly, it all started to make sense. He now understood why AJ knew so much about entrepreneurship and why he felt kindred to him. Like an unveiling of a great painting, it was now obvious to him, and he wondered why he hadn't seen it before. As the shock began to wear off, Luke started to feel deeply excited and relieved that he wasn't meeting the infamous Mr. Stanton. Instead, he'd be spending time with a man he cared about and respected.

For two hours, they ate, drank, and laughed. Almost like a bonus round, Luke was grateful to spend time with the two men who had guided him on the trip. Though slightly embarrassed about misjudging AJ, he realized that they weren't offended and truly appreciated Luke for his candid conversations.

After they finished, they traveled to the balcony that overlooked the pool and adjacent lake. Three large loungers with side tables provided an ideal spot to enjoy the cool breeze blowing off of the water.

As Luke sat down, he exhaled a deep breath and said, "So what's next for us, gentlemen? What's on the agenda for tomorrow?"

"Well, Miguel's got to be headed home to his family, and you and I are going fishing. We've got business to discuss, and I want to make sure you fully understand the *EntreSpirit*," AJ said.

For the next twenty minutes, the men sat in silence, enjoying the views of the water and the twinkling stars above. It made for the perfect ending to an emotional day. Closing his eyes, Luke thought back to how he had started the journey. Only a week ago, his life seemed so different. Remembering how he laid face down on his boat, wailing like a baby, made him quietly laugh at himself. He'd lost his friend, company, and was being sued for everything he owned, but that didn't seem to bother him as much anymore. The truth is, something had shifted deep inside of Luke, and regardless of how the contest ended, he knew he was going to be okay.

16 FISHING FOR THE ENTRESPIRIT

Before the sun was even up, Luke and AJ had breakfast and said goodbye to Miguel. After loading up a cooler with the men's lunches, two travel cups of coffee were brewed, and the men headed to the dock behind AJ's home. Boarding a small fishing boat, they motored a short distance to one of AJ's favorite fishing spots, known for its largemouth bass. Pulling up along the bank, AJ cast his line in the reeds. Before Luke could even bait his hook, AJ began to reel in his first fish. It was a small one, but Luke immediately realized he was fishing with a pro.

"How do you think you did this week?" AJ started the conversation as he released his catch back into the water.

After taking a sip of his coffee, Luke responded as he cast his line. "I don't know. Besides thinking the boss was a recruiter, I think I did okay. I had a good time anyway."

"Good! I'm glad you enjoyed yourself. We all think really well of you, Luke," AJ said. "Tomorrow morning, I'm going to give you our decision on the contest, but today, I'd like to dig through what you learned and want to ask you a few questions. Tell me what you think about the *EntreSpirit*. Do you think you possess the principles you learned about this week?"

Luke slowly began to reel in his line as he carefully considered AJ's words. "Honestly, I'm not sure what I have. I know I have something, I'm just not sure what it is."

"Well, let's discuss it then, starting with your mission. Remember, M-O-V-E-S. The M stands for mission. What did you discover about having a mission?" AJ prodded Luke in hopes he'd remember.

Luke thought for a moment and then said, "When we went to Peru and met the missionary there, I have to admit that I didn't think of him as entrepreneurial. As you shared his story though, I realized he had a purpose for his life and his mission drove him. The big takeaway from that story is that entrepreneurs are everywhere—not just in business. In regard to CataSail, I can see now that we lacked a mission. We just built boats to make money, but there was no real passion behind our work."

AJ responded by repeating the statement connected to principle one, "**The *EntreSpirit* serves a MISSION, working for a purpose far greater than financial gain, power, or success. Its motivation comes from a strong conviction that they were born to make a difference in the world.** Don't beat yourself up though! Sometimes it takes a while to find your mission. And there's nothing wrong with making money in business—actually, making money is pretty important! Just remember, the mission is the why. It has to be bigger than the enticement of money and should almost feel like a higher calling. It's your purpose and what's going to keep you moving forward when the going gets tough. And what about O—overcoming? What did you learn from Aaron at the baseball game?"

After taking a moment to process AJ's words, Luke recast his line along the bank and began to answer. "That guy kicked my butt! Let's see though. When I think back to my time running CataSail, I don't think I understood overcoming—at least not in the way that you and Aaron explained it to me. Somehow, I naively believed that we would never fail. More than that, I didn't create a culture where setbacks were expected or appreciated as part of the process. I've missed it too. I've thought a lot about what you said the other day, and I can see that I took CataSail's loss too personally. I overidentified with it, and it's kept me down for far too long."

AJ felt a bite and quickly jerked the pole to set the hook. Missing the catch, he groaned and then continued, "That's a good observation. **The *EntreSpirit* OVERCOMES. It considers setbacks and failures as part of the journey. Its relentless work ethic and commitment to win allow it to move forward despite adversity.** Every entrepreneur worth their salt will have failures, setbacks, and ideas that miss their mark. Life is hard and there will always be accidents and things we don't expect. That's why we have to anticipate adversity and be prepared to overcome it. Allowing room for setbacks is also healthy for a company's culture. It allows people to be creative, to try new things, and to make adjustments along the way. What you've experienced with CataSail and your partner passing were terrible losses, but those hurts will make you a better man as you move forward with determination to overcome."

Putting another worm on his empty hook, Luke nodded and asked, "You go fishing very often?"

"Maybe once a month or so, which isn't as often as I'd like. It's one of my favorite things to do when I need to think. Which reminds me, tell me about Dr. Torres, your host from Seattle. What did she teach you about the importance of having a clear V—vision?"

"Yes, Dr. Torres...well, she helped me see that our vision had become stale and outdated. Also, I'd become so busy that I didn't have time to even think through what we were doing anymore. I remember when we started CataSail, Dellin and I would sit for hours trying to figure out some new technologies. I'd even come up with new ideas in my sleep. But as we grew larger, we both got so busy running the company that we didn't have time to think about our vision. I pushed for growth without clarity. We were moving our location, expanding operations, and pushing ahead, but now I can see that nobody was clear about what we were doing or where we were headed."

"Right!" AJ said. "That's why you needed a fresh vision. The vision is a clear picture of what your company aims to do and how you plan to do it. Remember, **the *EntreSpirit* has VISION. It consistently thinks and daydreams about the future. It takes what seems invisible to others and turns it into reality.** Actually, what happened at your company is pretty normal. When any organization starts to mature, it becomes increasingly easy to lose focus and get off track. You get so busy that you forget what you're doing and why you're doing it. That's why you have to keep your vision in front of you. You also have to continually go back and make adjustments to it, thinking through details so that it stays current and relevant. Does that make sense?"

"It does, sir," Luke said as he recast his line. "When Dr. Torres explained daydreaming, I thought she was joking at first. But after she shared what went into creating Disneyland, I realized that when you have a big vision with a lot of details, it's also going to take plenty of thinking. Unfortunately, I barely thought about our vision. I became so consumed in my work that our vision moved to the wayside, and I was working on ideas that no longer mattered."

"That's a good perception, Luke," AJ said. "Now, let's talk about Tulo and your pursuit of education. He was proud of you for pushing him and asking about the *EntreSpirit*. It showed curiosity and a desire to learn. What did you learn about E—education?"

After thinking about AJ's question, Luke responded carefully. "I don't think I understood where he was going with his questions at first. It felt like he was provoking me. Then it felt like he was calling me an idiot and that my formal education was worthless—that ticked me off. But as he spoke about continuing my education as an adult, I realized where he was coming from. He made some great points, and as I've thought about it more, I agree with him. Most of the things I've had to master in life came after college. I learned from seminars, mentors, books, and asking questions. Heck, a lot of what I learned was from getting it wrong and then figuring out the right way."

AJ smiled and added, "Good! Business, just like life, is stretching. It's a hurricane. Most people don't realize how hard it will be when they get started. You've got to learn about leadership, finance, human resources, marketing, and management. They may teach you the basics in school—if you're lucky—but you have to know a lot more than that to win. Winning only comes from being over your head and learning how to swim in the deep end. Remember that your education isn't just reading books, but it's the pursuit of useful knowledge. It can come in many different forms. **The *EntreSpirit* continually EDUCATES itself. Its ferocious appetite for useful information causes it to continue learning throughout its lifetime."**

Finally, Luke's line took a huge hit. It surprised him so much that he nearly dropped the pole as the line began to run. Luke came alive, letting out a howl of excitement as he tried to reel it in. AJ set down his poll and hopped on the trolling motor to help Luke get in position. For nearly three minutes, Luke fought the monster until finally, he was close enough. Passing his pole to AJ, Luke leaned over the boat, carefully pulling up the largest bass he'd ever caught in his life. By AJ's fishing scale, it was 13.9 pounds—bigger than any bass AJ had ever seen or caught.

After a quick picture, Luke released the fish back into the water, talking to it as if it were a child and thanking it for biting his line. Turning to AJ, he decided to joke with his friend and said, "It's all in the wrist. You gotta make 'em feel like it's really moving through the water. If you're interested, I can give you some lessons. Remember, E stands for education."

AJ shook his head in disgust. "Well, L stands for luck, and that's all that was! Even a blind man can catch a fish once in a while." The men both laughed as they baited their hooks again in hopes of catching the next fish.

AJ continued the discussion and said, "So let's review. You understand M—Mission, O—Overcoming, V—Vision, and E—Education. Tell me about S—Satisfaction. What did you learn from Fred, our writer in North Carolina?"

Luke slowly reeled in his line. Turning to AJ, he said, "Fred is probably one of the most interesting people I've ever met. At first, I thought he had a bad case of ADHD, but as we settled into a conversation, he became more focused and offered a wealth of information. He helped me more than he'll probably ever realize. In hindsight, I thought I loved CataSail, and closing the company was one of the hardest things I've ever faced. Fred helped me see that it wasn't the company that I loved. What I loved was working on my creation—not because I'm a workaholic, but because it didn't feel like work at all. It was a joy for me because I found satisfaction in what I was doing."

AJ nodded and smiled, seeming to be very pleased with Luke's responses. "Exactly! When you love what you do, you'll never feel like you're working. It will be hard at times, and you'll get tired, but if you love it, it shouldn't feel like treacherous work. **The *EntreSpirit* finds great SATISFACTION in its work, often leading to seasons of imbalance. Internally driven to achieve, it enjoys its creation and watching it grow**. There are some pitfalls to this, and you have to find a healthy work-life balance, but few people truly know what it is like to be satisfied with their work. You did good, Luke, we're all really proud of you. Excellent job!"

Luke nodded and said, "Well, I'm thankful to you and all your hosts. I feel like the lessons I learned this week were very helpful in my situation. I even feel a little bad for getting paid to join you."

AJ laughed. "I'll take that check back if you'd like?"

"I don't feel that bad," Luke responded with a smile. "I am curious about something though. You keep saying that I've done well this week, and you're all proud of me. Honestly, I feel like I've been a big pain in the butt at times. There have been moments when I've disagreed with you and the hosts. As I've started to understand the *EntreSpirit*, I realize that I certainly haven't lived it. I mean, I've missed it with a lot of these principles. So, how can you say I've done well?" As Luke spoke, he surprised himself that he didn't take his shortcomings personally. Instead, he was being vulnerable, simply acknowledging the facts of his past.

Unmoved by Luke's words, AJ said, "We all fall short at times, son! Don't be too hard on yourself. To answer your question though, we believe you've done well for one simple reason. You've been teachable. When we tested you, we found that you were willing to learn."

"Tested me?" Luke asked.

AJ continued, "Yes...we tested you. This past week, you've had the privilege of meeting Stanton Enterprises' board of directors. But they're more than that—they're all very good friends of our family. We've asked them to be on our board because they all have the *EntreSpirit* and deeply understand the principles we value. I trust their judgments, and if you can make it through all of them, it shows us that you're teachable."

"I don't think I understand," Luke said as he slowly reeled in his empty line. "This was all to see if I'd be teachable?"

AJ nodded as he turned to Luke. "Doesn't that make sense? We have thirty-two corporations, but you didn't meet any of those leaders. On Monday, we dragged your butt deep into the Amazon jungle. We pelted you with rain and expected you to learn a business truth from a missionary. On Tuesday, you visited Aaron at the baseball game. He pushed all of your buttons in a way that only he can do—and you didn't crack. I know that must have been hard, but you made it through. When I shared with you their stories and the valuable lessons they held, you listened to me—even though you thought I was a recruiter. Honestly, how many people do you think would endure the first two days?"

Luke didn't answer. Instead, he shrugged his shoulders and turned in his seat to face AJ, now fully engaged in his words.

AJ continued his explanation. "Let me just tell you, I've seen some of our toughest contestants give up after those first two days. But you made it through the whole week. On Wednesday, you met a doctor, not a business leader, who talked to you about daydreaming and creating margin for your vision. On Thursday, Tulo quizzed you for twenty minutes and then pounced on you, telling you that your prestigious degree was practically worthless. Lastly, you met Fred, who appears extremely hyper, eccentric, and not what most would consider put-together at all. Yet, through all of this, you still were willing to learn something. That's why we're proud of you. You were willing to learn from others."

"All the hosts were unique, that's for sure. I won't say it was easy, but I did find each of them and what they shared interesting. So, you're saying that some contestants aren't willing to learn?" Luke asked.

"That's exactly what I'm saying. Some of them board the plane and the reek of arrogance is obvious. They demand a special menu, special drinks, and boss Miguel around like he is their personal assistant. By the time I have a conversation with them, they're already telling me how we should run the contests. They're so arrogant that they completely dismiss the valuable lessons taught by our hosts. When we push their buttons, some of them get so offended that they demand to go home early. You asked me the other day about what disqualifies contestants. I'll tell you right now that the number one reason is being unteachable—and all of that is a result of pride," AJ said passionately.

"Pride?" Luke questioned.

"Yes. Pride. It's the antithesis of the *EntreSpirit,* and where there is pride, the *EntreSpirit* can't exist. You have been through an incredibly challenging week of testing. During this extended interview, we've put you in positions to learn your character, personality, and stretch you. You could have given up, but you didn't. You've been humble and willing to learn, even though it was hard," AJ answered.

Luke didn't respond right away as he reeled in his line and reached for another worm. He thought back to some of the arrogant customers from his days at CataSail, and he imagined them going through the contest. Chuckling to himself, he realized that most of them wouldn't have made it past the first day. Luke now understood that the contests were more than just lessons that taught the company's principles. They were interviews conducted outside the confines of an office, created to learn the true character of the contestants and expose the arrogant.

Realizing the genius of the process, Luke said even more humbly, "I think I understand where you're coming from, sir. I remember having customers from time to time that wanted the perfect boat. They came in with a long list of requirements and demands. They were so arrogant and wouldn't stop to listen for five minutes about what was even possible. I even remember this one guy that walked out of a meeting because we told him his boat would sink if we used his required material list."

Without turning to Luke, AJ responded as he cast his line again. "That's a great example. Humility and teachability are synonymous with the *EntreSpirit*. Pride, on the other hand, is at the opposite end of the spectrum. Think about it like this. When someone is full of themselves, how is there room for a mission that serves others? There isn't! They will only do what is best for themselves. Secondly, their pride forces them to cover up their mistakes and act like they have everything together. They'll never admit they need to overcome something because they won't admit to any shortcomings. In regard to having a vision, it takes great humility to make adjustments along the way. For that to happen, they have to admit they don't have it figured out or that something isn't working. When someone thinks they already know everything, they're not going to pursue meaningful education. Why should they? They already know it all! Lastly, they'll never enjoy their work or find true satisfaction in it. No! They're always comparing their work to someone else's. In short, when someone is full of pride, they're disqualified immediately. We've found that the best contestants, and our top-performing entrepreneurs, are all confident and strong but are also very teachable."

"So, they need to be humble but still have a healthy ego?" Luke asked genuinely.

AJ smiled at Luke, appreciative of his question and interest in the subject. After taking a few seconds to consider it, he answered, "Let me see how I can explain this better. The *EntreSpirit* is humble but not like most would expect. It isn't weak or puny. By nature, it is full of confidence and has a healthy self-image. It's strong and secure, so it doesn't need to compare itself to others for validation. The *EntreSpirit* has a mission bigger than itself, and its mission serves a greater good. It also freely makes mistakes because it doesn't care about perfection or what others think. It's vulnerable because it knows that the setbacks it faces will be good lessons, and it will overcome those setbacks. It adapts its vision, acknowledging that micro-changes are needed to achieve the best results. It's humble enough to realize that it doesn't know everything, so it goes through life learning and becoming better. It is content with its work because it simply wants to be the best version of itself. Do you see how the embodiment of the *EntreSpirit* is different from pride and arrogance?"

Luke listened intently as he examined his own life. Like a missile targeted towards his heart, AJ's words made a direct impact. It was now clear that pride and arrogance had derailed him at times as he reflected on his leadership of CataSail.

Luke vocalized his emotions as he processed them out loud. "What's sad is what you've just described is not how I've always handled myself. Looking back, I see that I did a lot of things out of pride. I guess I didn't realize there was a different way."

AJ turned in his seat, placing his pole down. Looking at Luke, he gave him the warmest of smiles and said, "Don't be discouraged, son. In the last couple of years, you've been through some heavy stuff, and it's taught you some valuable lessons. Right now, it doesn't feel good, but it's going to help you when you get to the other side."

"Other side of what?" Luke asked, unsure of what AJ meant.

AJ hooked another fish, but it was another small one. Slowly reeling it in, he explained, "The other side of all you've faced in the last couple of years. You see, facing hard times is good for your soul because it can keep you humble and teachable, that is, if you allow it to. Your hard times enabled you to be here this week and admit you don't have it all together. You came in with an open mind, ready to learn, and that's why you've done so well this week. Nobody likes facing adversity—it's painful! But as you rebuild your life, your confidence is gonna return. You already have the skills to be successful, so now it's just a matter of time. The *EntreSpirit* will come to life inside of you and you're going to do great. I'd bet on it!"

Luke put his pole down and said, "Thanks for the encouragement, AJ. But I don't understand what you just said about the *EntreSpirit*—it isn't something you either have or don't have? It has to come to life?"

"The *EntreSpirit* is simply the DNA of self-starters and people who get things done. It isn't determined by your employment status, career choice, or position in a company. People have the *EntreSpirit* in every race, cultural background, and nationality. You're not actually born with it though, and you don't catch it like a fish. You see, the *EntreSpirit* is a path you choose in life. It's a decision made on the inside. Will you live and work with a mission? When it gets hard, are you determined to overcome? Will you dream and keep your vision fresh and relevant? Are you committed to your education and personal growth? Are you pursuing something that gives you deep satisfaction? If you can say yes to those questions, then you're living by the principles of the *EntreSpirit*."

For the next three hours, the men continued to fish and discuss life. Desiring to be completely authentic, Luke shared unashamedly about the lawsuit from JROB Holdings and the many adversities he was facing. AJ didn't seem concerned. Instead, he poured out wisdom and hard truth—almost like what a good father would do. He encouraged Luke to make amends with the investors and try to work out a deal. If that didn't work, filing bankruptcy was always an option. Hearing AJ's wisdom and willingness to help, Luke moved the conversation to marriage and raising kids. He could have sat and listened to AJ all day, but time was running out, and after lunch, the men headed back to the house.

AJ's wife had just returned home from a trip visiting their grandkids, and he was excited to see her. That night, the couple decided they'd go out for dinner. Though AJ's wife politely offered for Luke to join them, he didn't feel like it was right. Besides, Luke saw the relief on AJ's face when she asked and he declined. For the better part of one week, AJ had invested in Luke, and it was only fitting for him to have some time with his wife. Furthermore, Luke was mentally and emotionally exhausted. After a quiet dinner alone, he called home. He tucked his kids into bed by video and even sang them their favorite good night song. Afterward, he talked to his wife for hours, explaining the mysteries of his trip and all about the ginormous fish he'd caught.

As Luke lay on his bed that night, it was hard for him to fall asleep. It had been a crazy week, but he was thankful for everything that had happened. Though he learned some valuable lessons from each of his hosts, AJ had taught him something deeply profound and a new sense of confidence came over him. Luke vowed to live by the principles of the *EntreSpirit* and that if he ever started another business, he'd do it the *EntreSpirit* way. He didn't know what his mission would be, but it would be deeply personal. His mindset would be that of an overcomer who accepted small setbacks as part of the journey. His vision would be fluent and clear, and he'd make time to think. He'd continue to grow and educate himself daily. Lastly, he'd pick something that he loved dearly and that brought him satisfaction.

17 AN ENTRESPIRITED OPPORTUNITY

By seven o'clock, the smell of fresh bacon filled Luke's bedroom. Sitting in the room's easy chair, Luke sighed as he looked down at his watch. It was early, but he had already been up for a couple of hours rehearsing various speeches. The thought of winning the contest now deeply excited him. AJ was a man of integrity and becoming one of his CEOs would mean a fresh start. He'd probably get to see Miguel fairly often as well. Considering all of this, he carefully recited his speech to thank AJ.

"Thank you, AJ. I really appreciate your belief in me. I know we got off to a rough start, but this week was a turning point in my life. I'm very excited about this opportunity, and I won't let you down," Luke said under his breath.

He shook his head—it sounded so cheesy. And just as Luke's hopes were lifted that he might win, doubts crept in, causing him to practice a different speech. "That's okay, AJ. I can understand why I might not be a good fit for running the company. I have strong opinions, and it probably wouldn't have worked out well. I appreciate your consideration and wish you the best in the future," he said again in a whisper.

Taking a deep breath, Luke tried to settle his nerves. Which one of AJ's businesses needed a CEO? Maybe it was something in technology? Maybe real estate? After all, Luke had owned quite a few properties over the years. But could Luke handle it? Maybe he wasn't supposed to win. Maybe he just came here to refocus and get ready for a new venture. After all, he wouldn't have a controlling interest in AJ's company and he'd have a board to answer to. On the other hand, he didn't have any other options. JROB Holdings was breathing down his neck, and he needed something to do.

Standing up, Luke said, "It's game time. Whatever's going to happen is going to happen. Roll with the punches. Be tough!" Then he walked out the door, suitcase in tow.

When Luke reached the dining room, he found it empty. Unsure of where to go, he followed the smell of bacon into the kitchen. A young man, probably in his mid-twenties, was at work preparing breakfast and quickly waved his hand for Luke to enter. He pointed towards another door and simply said, "AJ's waiting at the breakfast table for you, sir."

As he opened the door, Luke was pleased to discover a part of the house he'd never seen. Almost like a Florida room with floor-to-ceiling glass windows, it offered an amazing view of the lake. Sunlight flooded the room, making the four-top table and chairs seem cheerful. Completing the room were two small sofas that faced each other, separated by a plush rug and gas fireplace along the wall.

"Good morning, young man! How's it feel to be headed home today?" AJ said from the table.

"Good morning, sir," Luke responded. "It feels pretty good. I'm looking forward to sleeping in my own bed and seeing my family."

"I bet you are! Grab a seat, and let's get started," AJ added. "How do you like the view?"

"It's nice. I haven't seen this room yet. I like it," Luke answered.

"This is Mrs. Stanton's favorite room, and if she has it her way, which she probably will, the entire house is going to get painted white and decorated like this. Anyway, we love eating breakfast here, and I asked her to let us use this room this morning. So, let's get right to it. We've had a busy couple of weeks, and this round of competition was tough. We can't invest in everyone, and there's a gal out of New Jersey that outperformed everyone. She's really something else!"

AJ paused as the young chef entered the room with the men's breakfast and set the table. The time he spent uncovering their plates and pouring their coffee gave Luke time to digest AJ's words. It sounded like he'd just lost the contest. His anxiousness wouldn't allow him to wait for the man to leave. He couldn't. Instead, he blurted out, "So this lady won the contest?"

AJ didn't answer right away. Instead, he waited for the young man to finish. After thanking him, he smiled at Luke and said, "Yes, she's our top choice for this round. But that doesn't mean you lost. We're actually considering both of you for the next step."

"Okaaaay," Luke said, trying to make sense of the situation. "But I thought contests have winners and losers."

AJ nodded and said, "Oh, there are some losers all right. It's been an interesting couple of weeks, that's for sure. But this isn't about them, this is about you! Are you ready to hear about what comes next?"

"Yes, sir!" Luke said, curious about what AJ was presenting.

"We've decided to consider both of you for our CEO roles. We believe you both have what it takes, and the good news is that we have enough capital to invest in both of you. What I need you to do is go home and come up with your business plan. Take your time and make the plan perfect before you pitch us. But there are some caveats we need to discuss first."

Though AJ's words sounded positive and encouraging, Luke wasn't connecting the dots. His words bypassed his brain as he spoke out loud, "Business plan? For what?"

AJ chuckled and responded, "I don't know, son. You're the one with the *EntreSpirit*! Whatever you want it to be!"

Luke shook his head trying to make sense of AJ's words. "So, this isn't for the role of CEO at one of your existing companies? I must have missed that!"

AJ continued to chuckle. "Well, you might have assumed that was the case, but that's not how our contests work. First of all, it would be unwise to make you the CEO of one of our current companies. Remember, M—mission. You'd have to be deeply passionate about that company's mission. Honestly, it's pretty rare for us to have turnover with our CEOs anyway, and even if we did need to replace someone, there's plenty of people with the *EntreSpirit* inside of each company. These people have the same mission and could easily take over. This would be for something brand new. Something you care about. Does that make sense?"

"It does. I guess I—" Luke said and then paused to think. "Maybe you should just tell me everything, and then I'll let you know if I have any questions."

"That's usually best, son," AJ said, smiling.

After taking a bite of his eggs and washing it down with his coffee, he continued. "We invest in people first and in business ideas second. Now, your idea has to be a good one, but it doesn't have to revolutionize the world. It could be something as simple as a new restaurant chain with a hook. It could be a service that you innovate, a product launch, or a combination of both. The big thing is that it has to be something that you fully understand and are confident you could pull off. The numbers must also make sense. However, they need to be conservative, which isn't normal for a business plan."

Luke started to interrupt but pulled himself back. AJ could see Luke's wheels turning and paused to give him space to ask a question. Luke then asked, "So what kind of numbers are we talking about—revenue targets, margins, and seed capital?"

AJ nodded, confirming the question was good. "I have a document that covers all of that information for deals like this. I'll send it to you, but for now, I'll give you the highlights. Ideally, we're looking for you to build a business that can eventually hit fifty million in annual revenues.

It can be more or less, but we want conservative numbers. Revenues are not our biggest concern though. Our main objective is profitability. We'd like the company to become profitable or at least break even within twenty-four months, so you've got to be focused on turning things over quickly. In regard to seed capital, how much will you need to grow and make a profit? We want you to ask for enough to fund the growth and cover your expenses until the company turns profitable. That would be phase one of funding. Once you hit your goals, you'll find that our investors are extremely generous and will give you great terms if your progress continues."

"So let me make sure I understand you correctly. All I have to do is go home and come up with a winning business plan for anything I want? If I comply with the numbers and you like the plan, it gets funded? It's that easy?" Luke asked, trying to confirm AJ's words.

"Nothing's easy about business!" AJ said after taking another sip of his coffee. "You'll have to come and pitch your idea to us, and I can't guarantee we'll fund your project. I will tell you that we fund over 70 percent of the ideas pitched to us from our winners, so your odds are pretty good."

In the many years of being CEO of CataSail, Luke had thought of hundreds of new business ideas. Now, as he ate breakfast with a billionaire who offered him a blank check, he couldn't think of a single one. How could he? His mind raced to keep up with AJ's words, who continued the conversation. For the next ten minutes, AJ shared the specific details of the offering, including equity positions, stock classifications, salaries, and financial accountability. AJ's tone was serious and demanded respect.

"If we fund your business, you'll become one of our founders and will be part of our *EntreSpirit* family. We have gatherings a couple of times a year, and you'll be expected to join us. Besides, we'd love to meet your wife and family. These get-togethers are always a fun time, and you'll get to connect with some wonderful people," AJ continued.

"That wouldn't be a problem. I'd love to meet them," Luke said assuredly.

"But that's not all, Luke. You'll have to run the business based on the principles you learned this week. You'd have to do it the *EntreSpirit* way. Mistakes and setbacks won't get you fired—remember, we are open to failures and are prepared to overcome them. What will get you fired is ignoring the *EntreSpirit* principles. When you pitch us, you'll need to present more than a plan to make money. We need to believe that the mission deeply matters to you—if it doesn't, we'll be able to sniff that out and we'll push back on you. Understood?" AJ continued his tone. He was respectful to Luke, but he wasn't the warm, encouraging man who'd lifted Luke's spirits a couple of nights before. Instead, he was in full-on investor mode.

"Yes, sir! Understood. I'll keep digging in! M-Mission, O-Overcoming, V-Vision, E-Education, and S-Satisfaction," Luke confirmed, reciting the MOVES acrostic.

AJ continued, "Besides having a mission, we expect you to be tough. There are going to be setbacks along the way. Something's going to come up that you didn't expect. We want you to own it, and then figure out how to overcome it! Your business plan is only the starting point of your vision. You'll have to discipline yourself to work less and think more. Every day, we want you to take at least an hour to think through your vision and solve big problems. We expect you to educate yourself and continue to grow. You'll need to keep reading and learning every day. And lastly, you need to pick something you love and that gives you great satisfaction."

Again, the young man entered the room. Quietly, he refilled the men's coffee cups and removed the empty plates and silverware. After thanking him, AJ continued with a final requirement. "There's one more thing, Luke. It's not just you who needs the *EntreSpirit*. If you're the only entrepreneur in your company, you'll never reach your full potential. To really hit the ball out of the park, you need to make sure the *EntreSpirit* is deeply rooted in your team and culture. Every leader needs to see themselves as an entrepreneur and owner of your company. They'll have the same mission. They're tough overcomers. They'll own the vision for their department. They're pursuing education. And more than anything, they're satisfied and love coming to work every day. If you can accomplish that, you're going to be incredibly successful."

AJ wiped his mouth with the napkin that had been left on the table. He seemed to be finished with the guidelines, and Luke now thought it was appropriate to ask a question.

"AJ, the other day, you mentioned a contestant that won, but he didn't end up partnering with you. I don't understand how anyone could be offered something like this and not be interested?"

"Right. So now you're going to go home and come up with a big idea. Heck, you'll probably have a couple of them. You've then got two options. You can come back here and pitch us on the idea. You'll be the CEO but won't have a controlling interest in the company. Your other option is to take that million-dollar check and go do it yourself. But as you told me, a million bucks ain't what it used to be!" AJ said as he chuckled.

"You've had contestants do that?" Luke asked curiously.

"You'd be surprised. Now, I've got about twenty minutes left with you before you need to catch a plane. Tell me if there is anything else you want to know. I want to make sure we cover everything," AJ's demeanor now returned to the friendlier version Luke had met earlier.

"I do have some questions, sir. So, all of these people I met this week—I mean, the hosts—I know they are your board of directors, but are they investors too? Is this your money, or is this like a venture capitalist type of deal?"

"Ah! That's a good question. Yes, some of our hosts do invest, but not all of them. Our investment money comes mostly from myself and other private angel investors looking to diversify. I wouldn't consider us to be venture capitalists though because they typically want very large returns and a quick exit strategy. We focus more on long-term sustainability and profitability. More of a get-rich-slowly formula. That is all covered in the documentation, and I can share more about that later if you end up pitching us."

It was obvious to Luke that AJ understood his stuff. Deciding to move on to a different topic, Luke thought through his curiosities. Slowly he began to speak, trying to phrase his words just right. "How did you get into all of this? And why are you involved in these contests? I mean, I am very glad that you spent so much time with me. I just didn't expect it. Seems like it would be easier to hire someone to be a guide."

"Well, those are some loaded questions, but I like what you're asking," AJ said as he put down his coffee cup. "I don't have to fly all over the map doing contests. I do it because I love it. Remember, satisfaction is part of the *EntreSpirit*, and if you love what you do, you'll never work a day in your life. I love spending time with entrepreneurs. For me, it's seeing their faces light up when they start to understand these principles. Then, they go home and think up some amazing new ideas. We've funded a lot of them, and they're fulfilling their dreams. It's very rewarding for me."

Luke nodded, thinking about how the opportunity might change his destiny as well.

AJ continued, "The truth is, I'm retired. But is any entrepreneur ever really finished? Eight years ago, I had a fella pitch me an idea. He wanted a hundred grand to start a business. I could see right away that he didn't have what it takes, so I started thinking about the DNA of entrepreneurs and what I'd invest in. Over the years, I've known a lot of successful entrepreneurs, so I began to ask them for insight as well. That's how we came up with the *EntreSpirit*. One thing led to another, and here I am today. It's not like I'm working hard though. We'll do these contests for a couple of weeks, and then I'll relax until someone comes along with a business plan. It's a fine set-up for an old guy like me."

Luke smiled at AJ and said, "It's pretty remarkable, and it does sound like a lot of fun. So, what did you do before you retired? Until Friday, I thought you were in human resources, so there are a few gaps for me."

AJ chuckled and said, "Well, let's see here. Most of my money came from oil. I was raised in Midland, Texas, and back then, everyone was big on oil. My daddy worked on a rig for most of his life. He felt like it would be good for me too, so I got into it when I was about seventeen. Before long I was leading a shift as a driller. But I wasn't content. I saw how much oil we were producing, how much it was worth, and compared that to my paycheck. I knew right then and there that I wanted to own a rig. That's when the entrepreneurial bug hit me. I got together with some guys I knew who were out of work, and I started a drilling company. I called up all the rich people I could find to see if they wanted a piece of the action, and we started hunting for oil. Well, I couldn't find oil to save my life. For two years, we burned through so much money and ticked all our investors off. That company eventually folded. So, when I tell you I understand hard times, I'm talking from personal experience."

"How did you pull out of that?" Luke asked.

"Well, it wasn't easy, that's for sure. I went back to work drilling. One day, I had a guy call me up who came into some money and wanted to invest, so we gave it another go. Thankfully, we hit it big on two rigs. We expanded to a couple more teams and kept growing. We sold those out years ago, and I've been mostly an investor over the years, but I know what it's like to get down and dirty too."

As Luke listened, he could envision a younger version of AJ working on oil rigs and conducting business. He smiled as he thought of him sweating in the Texas heat, a hardhat on his head, and a smudge of oil on his cheek. He was an old-school entrepreneur, born before the days of mobile phones and the internet. If AJ wanted something back then, he couldn't just do an internet search. Like oil, AJ had to dig for success. Wondering how he could have raised money back then, Luke imagined AJ dialing up investors on a rotary phone and driving to their houses to pitch them with a paper business plan. He probably stayed until they agreed, and then walked out with a check in hand. Luke's thoughts made him smile, and it encouraged him that regardless of age, the entrepreneur's spirit was kindred.

"Excuse me, sir. The car is here," a voice rang out from behind where Luke was sitting.

Regrettably, Luke's time with AJ had come to a close. As the men stood up, Luke began to express his gratitude once again with a few final words.

"AJ, I don't think I could ever thank you enough for how much you've helped me this week. You've been incredibly generous with your time. The truth is, I was in a very bad way and didn't know which end was up. However, you and all of your hosts invested in me. You showed me things in a different light and I'll always be grateful for that. I guess you could say your timing was sort of a miracle. All I can say is, thank you again, my friend."

AJ smiled as the men firmly shook hands and said, "You're welcome, it's been my pleasure, Luke. You've got a bright future ahead of you, and I'm excited to see how everything turns out. I hope to hear from you soon and learn about the ideas you come up with."

Of course, Luke would have liked to stay longer, but time simply wouldn't allow it—and just like that, his journey that spanned more than 14,000 miles was over. He'd met five interesting hosts and traveled in luxury high above the clouds. There all along were AJ and Miguel, guiding him on the adventure and encouraging him to search for something inside. Though buried in mud and sleeping deep below the surface of his heart, Luke could feel it emerging within him. It was the *EntreSpirit*. It had been there all along. Somehow, be it luck or fortune, he was found worthy of the contest. Somehow, despite his brokenness and scars, they saw value inside of him—something that even Luke couldn't see in himself.

As he headed to the car waiting outside, a quiet confidence slowly came over him, unlike anything he'd known before. For the first time in his life, everything about his personality and wiring became crystal clear. He understood why he felt different from others and why he was so driven, passionate, and creative. Though normal people might consider him insane, he knew he was far from crazy. He was simply an entrepreneurially-minded soul, a pioneer, and someone who wasn't content to live in the confinement of a box.

18 CHOOSING THE ADVENTURE

So, what happened to Luke? As I penned the pages of this book, I found myself conflicted about how this story might come to a close. In the end, I decided that some things are best left to one's imagination. I realize some readers want to know what happened to Luke and have everything tied up in a perfect little bow. However, that's not how life or entrepreneurship works. Though I can't give you all the details for the ending, one thing is certain—Luke's life was forever changed by the people he met on his journey. They each provided little nuggets of wisdom and encouraged him to think differently. I'm confident that Luke continued his life of entrepreneurship, but this time around, he would approach it in a new way.

I can see him on the plane ride home. Though he's physically and emotionally exhausted, I picture Luke doing some serious soul-searching. What was his mission? Could he solve a problem that he deeply cared about? Could his new business make a difference in the world? He'd had so many ideas over the years, and many of them seemed good at the time. Now, after understanding the *EntreSpirit*, one by one, they were eliminated as he thought about the five principles. This time he'd do something that mattered to him. His mission would be personal and something worth fighting for.

As he rides home from the airport, he's smiling from ear to ear. Unmoved by the stench of the little yellow taxi, he's feeling alive again. He sees the world in a different light and is determined to overcome adversity. Don't feel sorry for him because he doesn't feel sorry for himself. He's decided not to be a victim of his circumstances. Instead, he's charting his course for the upcoming week. He's ready to deal with the many issues surrounding the implosion of CataSail. On Monday, he'll start discussions with JROB Holdings. He's decided to move forward with whatever is needed to bring the CataSail fiasco to an end. Though nobody can say how the investors will respond, I believe Luke will handle himself well. And no, he won't be sleeping on his boat any longer. He'll probably take his attorney's advice and sell it, distributing the proceeds to his creditors and investors. Chances are good that he's going to lose his house and almost everything he owns, but you would never know it by the look on his face. He's now more confident and determined than ever.

As he walks into his house, his heart overflows as he hugs and kisses his wife passionately. The emotions continue to build as his children wrap around his legs, welcoming their father home. He kneels and embraces them as he touches their cheeks. Tears of joy pour from his face as he sees the beauty of his family. For the rest of the day, he sits with his wife by the pool, quietly telling her about the trip. They laugh and cry for hours, slowly reliving the journey together. Luke explains to Meredith how his lack of vision caused him to get caught up in meaningless tasks, taking him away from his family. He humbly apologizes for not being intentional and vows to live a more balanced life.

As the couple sits in bed that night, Luke carefully shares a new business idea with Meredith. What would she think? Would she be resentful after all he'd brought her through? She isn't. She's overjoyed to see her husband so excited about life and business again. At that moment, Luke realizes something that he's never seen before. Though it looks different in his wife's personality, she possesses the *EntreSpirit* too.

For the next two months, the couple works together with crystal clear focus. They sit and discuss their vision over breakfast every morning. Step by step, they knock out big and small tasks. For the first time in their lives, there is clarity to their vision. They immerse themselves in learning everything they can about their new idea. Packing their home up and preparing to move out should have been harder, but it wasn't. Instead, they talk about a new dream home as they listen to a podcast that encourages them to fight on. Their identity is no longer found in their belongings, but in the people they are becoming.

Did they take Stanton up on his offer? I don't know. The truth is, it doesn't really matter. With or without Stanton's investment capital, I believe Luke would still be profoundly successful. Deep inside of him, the *EntreSpirit* was coming alive, and it altered the view of his life and future. He no longer believed the lie that entrepreneurship was a psychotic killer, stripping him naked and leaving him for dead. Somewhere between the jungles of the Amazon and a country estate outside of Dallas, the blinders fell off. He was suddenly unshackled—the burden of failure and disappointment he carried was gone, and entrepreneurship had become beautiful again.

The truth is, entrepreneurship was never really the issue. The problem was how Luke had perceived it. He had believed it to be a metaphorical ladder one climbs to reach the top and where success awaits. But that's not reality. Like Luke's trip, entrepreneurship is a long journey to exotic places that most will never have the opportunity to experience. It's a constantly changing roller coaster ride, not meant for the timid or weak. There are seasons of adversity, where one travels uphill through rugged terrain. There are also financial pitfalls, jagged rocks, and deadly vipers along the way. Thankfully, there are also sweet seasons of prosperity and rest, where one sits and enjoys the fruit of their labor. Though not easy, entrepreneurship is a valuable and treasured journey, and to experience it is a reward in and of itself.

AFTERWORD
A LOOK INSIDE THE FABLE

This book is based upon some of the experiences and events my wife and I have faced during our twenty-year journey as entrepreneurs. To help readers understand the allegory and how I came up with Luke's adventure, I've decided to provide a few details.

Business Failures and Hardships

Luke's anguish in the first three chapters is reflective of the pain one may experience when entrepreneurial ventures go wrong. Our family experienced this pain for the first time in 2007 when our mortgage company folded—it was just six years old and was my passion. We had a spotless reputation, fifteen employees, and we were expanding as the housing bubble hit Florida. As the meltdown happened, I worked tirelessly to save the company—foregoing sleep and food in hopes of making it survive. It didn't, and during the aftermath, our family faced bankruptcy, foreclosure, and multiple lawsuits from business creditors. At thirty-one years old, I felt like a failure, and for a season, I struggled terribly with depression.

By the end of 2007, my wife and I launched a new company, offering specialized digital consulting for small businesses. Within twelve months, we restored our six-figure income and were enjoying newfound prosperity. Many people were surprised that we became successful again and began to ask me for training. For the next twelve years, we worked and expanded into a seven-figure consultancy and training business. The idea for CataSail's accident comes from a mix of two painful events that happened in the last couple of years before our consultancy closed. First of all, an overseas blogger negatively reviewed our training company online. Though he didn't know us and was never one of our customers, he painted a negative picture to divert sales from our company to his own product. We tried to get the content removed, but it was impossible due to his geolocation. As a result, our sales declined by nearly forty percent. What's worse is at the same time, my dear friend and college roommate suddenly passed away, causing tremendous grief for our family. Though my friend wasn't our cofounder, and he had a different personality than Dellin, his loss was immensely painful during this season.

Like CataSail, our training company also had investors. They weren't hard-nosed financiers from Wall Street but hard-working Americans. I hold them in the highest regard and will always be thankful for these wonderful men who believed in us. Luke's struggle to raise money after the accident also comes from personal experience. Just as our sales started to take a hit, we were in the process of raising capital. We received a commitment letter for a substantial cash infusion, but with declining revenues, the money never came. Sadly, after twelve years of business, we sold our assets, let go of our staff, and closed the company—resulting in financial losses for all involved. The first three chapters of this book reflect what entrepreneurs face every day when they take risks and lose. If you've ever suffered a business loss, no doubt you can relate to Luke's situation.

Luke's Journey

Luke's journey across the Americas symbolizes the entrepreneurial life. It is indeed the adventure of a lifetime—filled with unique characters and uncertainty. Even for the most driven and focused people, entrepreneurship can feel like Luke's trip. You don't know the destination, who you'll meet along the way, or how the contest will turn out, but you're excited to be on the plane.

The EntreSpirit

The five principles of the *EntreSpirit* are rooted in my twenty years of working with, training, and mentoring entrepreneurs. It all started when, at just twenty-five years old, I found myself training new loan officers at our mortgage business. The development of entrepreneurs continued during the twelve years that we trained people to start their own consulting agencies. Over the years, we've had the privilege of knowing and mentoring hundreds of people who desired the entrepreneurial life. Sarah and I are forever humbled to have had the privilege of knowing them, and we are extremely grateful for all that these men and women have taught us in return.

The Characters

The characters in the book are based upon various people I've met or observed through the years. Though the personalities in the book were created from my imagination, I believe they represent real-life people who have the *EntreSpirit*.

AJ/Stanton and Hosts - AJ and the hosts are a combination of the many good men and women who have spoken wisdom into my life over the years. Some of them have taught me from afar, sharing their wisdom through books and podcasts. Others have sat with me, sacrificing their time to help me learn and grow.

Miguel - Miguel represents the need for community, support, and encouragement along the entrepreneur's journey. He is sincere, warm, and unpretentious. Though entrepreneurs are usually self-driven adventurers, they still have moments of self-doubt and fear. I believe entrepreneurs become better when they have people like Miguel in their lives.

Luke - The easiest character for me to create was Luke Voightmann—because he symbolizes the best and worst parts of me. I think most entrepreneurs will find a piece of themselves inside of Luke's character as well.

Meredith and Family - I believe most entrepreneurs want to be good spouses and parents. However, sometimes we lose sight of what matters most due to the relentless pressure to achieve success. Meredith and Luke's children are valuable reminders of the importance of family and living a balanced life.

Hiring EntreSpirited Staff

Leading followers is easy! Leading the *EntreSpirited*—well, that's another story! Though it can be a tremendous challenge, there is nothing more rewarding than empowering another entrepreneur to take ownership of their role. It reduces the leader's burden and makes the entire organization better. I've seen firsthand that when leaders are trusted, empowered, and given ownership, they will thrive and be content to stay. I've also learned that when there is a lack of clarity or when they feel micromanaged, they will revolt. Over the years, I have had wonderful opportunities to learn these lessons by leading these strong men and women. Humbly, I'll admit that I've often led the wrong way. Writing this book has taught me so much and renewed my vision to become a better leader of the *EntreSpirited*.

Final Thoughts

The entrepreneurial journey has brought us tremendous seasons of joy and pleasure. Like Luke, our family has known the sweetness of success. At our peaks, we built two profitable companies that allowed us to experience the many wonderful blessings of life. We've had dream vacations, luxury cars, and expansive houses. I've experienced more joy and favor in my life over the last twenty years than I could have ever imagined.

However, the journey has also brought the bitter taste of bankruptcy, foreclosure, and losing material belongings. Nobody wants that. And certainly, no entrepreneur starts a business expecting it to fail. However, entrepreneurship is fierce and sometimes you get knocked down. Yes, those were painful seasons and we do have some gnarly scars to show. We're not embarrassed or ashamed of them. If anything, we're proud of our scars—they are constant reminders that we bravely faced adversity. Though we were wounded, we got back up and kept fighting.

Theodore Roosevelt once said, "Far better to dare mighty things, to win glorious triumphs, even though checkered by failure, than to take the rank with those poor spirits who neither enjoy much nor suffer much because they live in the gray twilight that knows not victory nor defeat."

The entrepreneur's life is uncertain—its pages to be written as time moves forward. There will be moments on your journey where you'll enjoy great success. You'll bet on yourself, defy the odds, and win! As Roosevelt suggested, there will also be setbacks along the way, and your wins will be checkered by failure. Don't give up! Never give up! Remember, you're not one of the poor spirits that live in the gray twilight of fear—you're an entrepreneur.

I hope this book has been an encouragement to you and as thought-provoking and healing as it has been for me to write.

FREE RESOURCES
TO HELP YOU REMEMBER THE PRINCIPLES

Thank you so much for purchasing and reading this book. As a small token of my appreciation, I've created a couple of free resources to help you keep the principles of the *EntreSpirit* in front of you. By scanning the QR code below with your smartphone, you'll be redirected to a private page on our website. There you'll find a few short videos explaining the *EntreSpirit* and how I came up with the story. Additionally, I've created a printable PDF document that lists the five principles of the *EntreSpirit*.

https://entrespirit.com/free-resources/

ACKNOWLEDGMENTS

Let me just tell you that writing a book takes a lot of time and hard work. Creating a story isn't enough though. After the book is complete, you have to get feedback, make edits, and finalize all the design content. I assure you that it is a long journey and you get weary along the way. The truth is, the *EntreSpirit* wouldn't exist without the help of some pretty amazing people. I'd be amiss if I didn't acknowledge them and their contributions.

First and foremost, I'd like to thank my wife, Sarah. When you first heard the story, you were so excited. You encouraged me to get up every morning and write until I finished. Once the first draft was completed (which was quite terrible) you spent your entire summer reading, editing, and making it so much better. Though you've read the book dozens of times, you never grew tired. Thank you so much for your continual support, affection, and kindness.

Secondly, I want to express my appreciation to our family members for their willingness to read and make the book better. Many thanks to our moms, Gail and Frances, for being our very first readers. You helped us develop characters and fix major plot holes. Also, special thanks to Liz for your wise feedback and for helping us improve Dr. Torres. To everyone else in our family who read the book, thank you for the many encouraging texts and conversations. It meant more than you probably ever realized and kept us moving forward.

Outside of our family, we asked two close friends to be our first beta readers. I'd like to especially thank Kristine, the beloved wife of my best friend who passed away in 2018. I know the story probably wasn't easy to read, but I thank you for your bravery and strength. When you finished the book in just a couple of days, it encouraged us so much! You took copious notes and gave us a very unique perspective. The story instantly became better because of your ideas and feedback. We love you and are praying for you!

Tom, you were our second beta reader and the first man to read the book. You're entrepreneurial-minded and a great leader. Honestly, I was so anxious as I waited for your feedback. The day you finished and blew up my phone with encouraging messages meant more than you could ever realize. Thanks for sitting with me on your porch to discuss the principles and answer my questions. When I left your house that day, I was so encouraged and couldn't wait to share the book with others.

After we completed the third draft, we needed more feedback. Could we get twenty *EntreSpirited* people to read the book? I wasn't sure, so I sent each of you a text message to see if you'd be interested in reading it. To my delight, you responded with anticipation. I printed each book at home and mailed you the manuscript. As each of you read the book, you encouraged us so much. I'm especially grateful to everyone who sat down with me and shared their suggestions. Thanks to my friends at the Journey, including Luke, Rob, and Jadner. You guys provided some great feedback and really grasped the principles in the book. You are all amazing leaders and I can't wait to see the impact you make. A big thanks to Tommy, Robert, and John, my FSMC brothers and fellow entrepreneurs. I'm so proud of all of you guys and how successful you've become. Thank you for your feedback and your great tips. There are other readers as well, but I'd specifically like to thank Tony, John, Patsy, Mike, and Danny. Without your encouragement, suggestions, and feedback, the book wouldn't have existed as it does today.

Acknowledgements

We also had some wonderful people that helped us finalize the book's appearance and copy. To Ian, our designer, I'm so thankful for your friendship. I'll always be grateful for the time we spent working together. You have a great future ahead of you and I see the *EntreSpirit* inside of you. We also had several freelance editors who provided feedback and helped us fix typos. Thank you to all of you for your input and ideas. I'd like to especially thank Yasmin for making everything perfect before print and publication.

Lastly, and most importantly, I'd like to thank God, my father in heaven. You were the one who gave me the strength, ideas, and ability to write this story. Without you, I am nothing. Your love for us is great and you truly make beauty out of ashes.

SHARING THE ENTRESPIRIT

In case you're wondering, it's our family's **MISSION** to encourage entrepreneurs. However, it's more than that. It's also our business. In 2021, we established MotusPress, a new publishing house committed to releasing helpful books for entrepreneurs. If you found this book valuable, we'd like to humbly ask for your help.

Share Your Story

First of all, we would love to hear from you. Tell us your story and what the *EntreSpirit* meant to you. We love meeting entrepreneurs and hearing their stories. You can connect with us by emailing us at stories@entrespirit.com.

Share in our Future

Are you interested in being one of our beta readers? Or do you want to be notified when our new books are released? You can stay in touch with all that's happening by joining our email list at https://entrespirit.com.

Share on Social Media

This is a big ask, but it would be incredibly helpful if you were willing to share our book with others on social media. To help with this, we created a special page on our website with social media graphics. Visit us at https://entrespirit.com/share to access everything. Don't forget to use the hashtag #ENTRESPIRITBOOK so we can thank you for posting!

Share a Review

Would you be willing to write a review? If so, it would mean the world to us. For a list of websites where you can review our book, just head over to https://entrespirit.com/reviews.

Share with Your Team and Others

Lastly, if you're interested in buying multiple copies for your company, team, or others, we have special bulk discounts available on our website. Please visit https://entrespirit.com/discount for more information.

Thank you again for your purchase and for partnering with us on our mission. We wish you the greatest success in the future!

Matt, Sarah, Libby, & Mattie Law

More Ways to Connect

Website   www.entrespirit.com
Twitter   twitter.com/mattlaw76
Facebook   facebook.com/mattlaw76
LinkedIn   linkedin.com/in/mattlaw76
Instagram   instagram.com/mattplaw76